HOW TO FIND THE
RIGHT ONE
&
MAKE IT LAST!

BRING LOVE AND ROMANCE
BACK TO DATING

HOW TO FIND THE RIGHT ONE

&

MAKE IT LAST!

BRING LOVE AND ROMANCE BACK TO DATING

CHARLES A. JOHNSON

Two Harbors Press
212 3rd Avenue North, Suite 290
Minneapolis, MN 55401
612.455.2293
www.TwoHarborsPress.com

ISBN-13: 978-1-937928-44-5
LCCN: 2012933382

Distributed by Itasca Books

Cover Design and Typeset by James Arneson

Printed in the United States of America

This book is dedicated to my mother, Ora Beatrice Johnson.

CONTENTS

FOREWORD

How to Find the Right One & Make It Last! is one of the most refreshing books I have read in a long time. If you are tired of trying to figure out the dating game and/or how to attract and keep true love, I highly recommend that you read this entire book. Both women and men can learn about the strategies that can bring romance and respect back to dating and/or more permanent relationships.

Dr. Deborah E. Johnson
Counselor and Personal Coach

PREFACE

*For over twenty-five years, I have been officially and unof-*ficially in the professional matchmaking business. I cannot say it was by choice; rather, it was something that needed to be done to help many of my single friends and colleagues. I have always concentrated on helping people achieve their professional dreams and have been quite successful. I have helped them achieve financial success, business and career success, new cars, new homes, money in the bank, etc. Yet inevitably, they would all come to me and say, "I have achieved all the professional success a man or woman could ever wish for, but I still feel like there's something missing in my life. I have all the trappings one could ever hope for, but I still feel like there has to be more to my life than professional success and accumulating wealth and things of pleasure. Since you have been my mentor I have achieved all I set out to do, but I need one more thing from you. I need you to help me find the right partner with whom to share my life and enjoy the future. I want some balance in my life and I think having someone special who truly loves and wants me in her [or his] life will help me accomplish this important goal."

I would always grimace and say, "But I am not in the matchmaking business. I am a business guy." They would look at me disappointingly and say, "I am depending on you to help me through this most difficult part of my life. As you know, I am extremely confident and competent in my professional life, but I do not have the same confidence, experience, skills, and competence in my personal life and especially in my dating life. I also heard that you've helped many others like me find their marriage partners."

One by one, I would sit them down and begin the transformation and transition required to help them develop a successful personal and private life. I still get chills when I see their faces when they finally find the right partner to marry and start to build a family together. It definitely takes some adjustment to balance their work and personal lives. In many cases, it requires learning a different set of skills to achieve success in their personal lives. For the last twenty-five years, I have helped hundreds of executive and professional women and men from around the world achieve personal and lasting relationship success. I think of them as my extended family. I want the same happiness for them as I have helped my own four children achieve in their lives. My former operations director, Victoria, and my beautiful wife, Pauline, inspired me to write this book. It is our collective hope that you will embrace the principles and concepts detailed in this book to transform your life, as Victoria has.

I helped Victoria transform her personal and professional life and showed her that she could have success in both areas. At the age of thirty-one, she already had accomplished amazing success in her work life, but she longed for the balance and love that she knew would come to her life when she found the right partner. With my help and coaching, Victoria did make that transition and found the perfect partner to complement her already successful life. Victoria also inspired me to build a company dedicated to helping single people transform their personal lives and achieve relationship success. My company is named AskDearlove Incorporated.

PREFACE

This book is based on the years of experience I learned through working with numerous professionals, executives, and our own four daughters. The book is also based on my life experiences, the real-world relationship experience of many of my successful married friends, extensive research, and simply observing what things work and what things do not work. I am confident that when it comes to finding and securing the right life partner, my time-proven techniques will work for you as well.

ACKNOWLEDGMENTS

I would like to express my deepest thanks to Victoria Adas, Stuart Broderick, Caroline Broderick, Giselle Ruiz, Jon Duckert, Paula Hamm, Debbie Johnson, Keith Johnson, Marilyn Johnson, Carolyn Herzog, Karen Dearlove, and my wife, Pauline Mary Dearlove Johnson, for their help with this book. Their insight, recommendations, and input were critical to the successful writing of this book and topic area.

INTRODUCTION

We all spend years learning how to become experts in our jobs, careers, and professions. We attend thirteen years of school and then go on to college or specialized schools to gain the knowledge we need to be competitive and successful in our chosen fields. But when we want to know where to go to find the required skills and experience to be successful in our personal lives, we often simply don't have an answer.

Some people are lucky enough to learn from their parents how to find the right partner and create a lasting relationship. But many of us come from broken homes or two-parent homes that do not mirror the life we have in mind. Also, many parents and older siblings simply do not share or teach the skills we need to build a successful personal life and relationship.

It seems odd that one of the most important success lessons we all need tends to receive the least amount of attention. We find ourselves wondering why we are having so little success with our personal and private lives. But many people just have not dedicated enough time to developing the skills for discovering the best places to look, nor have they determined what is best for them.

Many people are lucky or blessed enough to have found the perfect mate during their high school or college years, when they had a wide range of potential partners from which to choose. In school environments, you have a built-in social structure that tends to foster and nurture relationships. During this period of your life, you have access to classrooms full of interesting people, homecoming dances, house parties, field trips, study clubs, fraternities, sororities, football and basketball games—the list goes on and on. Some took advantage of this large social network and found the right partner. But many of those who placed less emphasis on finding the right partner during the school years—or perhaps just did not find the right person—are now wondering, "What do I do?"

Within the blink of an eye, you find yourself past your school years. Many of you have mastered the daily hustle and bustle of your work environment. You may even be considered one of the young lions or lionesses of your company. You are on the move! Your bosses have your name on the tip of their tongues. You have been groomed for a senior position in the company. You have status, the car, the nice condo, and money in the bank. People know your name at work; you are admired and you have reached or are about to reach the pinnacle of professional success. But no one realizes that every day of your successful life, you find yourself quietly asking, "What am I doing wrong? Why do I feel all alone and have no one with whom to share my special moments?"

Or you might be someone who is beginning your career, and you want to find someone to share your life. You look back on your school days and wonder why you didn't find the right one. You also might question whether there is something wrong with you. Self-doubt starts to creep into your thoughts, and you wonder if you are the only one having this issue.

Many people don't understand why they haven't found the right person. They tell themselves, "I know I am a good catch! There just doesn't seem to be enough of what I am searching for to choose from." They ask themselves, "Why do I keep attracting the jerks, the gold-diggers, the serial daters, the sex-crazed people, or the one who cannot accept and respect my job, my professional success, and my hard work?"—this can be particularly true for women.

After a while, we all start to figure out that even with all the professional success in the world, our work or career is simply not enough for us. Single professionals might say it is not necessary for them to be with a partner, a mate, a loved one, but I have found over the years of working with such people that they do miss the balance that comes from having someone at home who truly loves them. I believe that most people, deep down inside, would like to have that special person who gives them a reason to go home. Most of us imagine having someone with whom to share our special moments and celebrations. And above all, most people would like to have someone who brings that smile to their face and makes life a little more enjoyable.

This book is about providing answers to the questions:

1. How do I attract the right people?
2. Why can't I find the right person?
3. What changes do I need to make?
4. What skills and access am I missing?
5. What are men really looking for?
6. What are women really looking for?
7. Where do I look?

The goal of this book is to take the "what is wrong with me" worries away and replace them with hope, love, passion, and relationship success. It's never too late to find the right person and learn how to make your relationship work and last. This book will show you how to find someone who really cares about you and ignites the fires deep inside your soul. It is about taking your life to the next level and concentrating on your personal life and your happiness. The first step to making that happen is to recognize that *there's nothing wrong with you.*

There are literally tens of millions of people throughout the United States and the world who are just like you—single. In fact, there are over 104 million single people in the US alone, according to the 2010 US Census Bureau Report. That is over one-third of the US population. Many of you have already demonstrated that you are willing to work hard to achieve success in your work life. With a little more effort and a few new skills, you will be equally successful in your personal life. Now, that is something to get excited about!

Start thinking about yourself and what you want. And don't listen to people who offer advice but do not live the professional and personal life you want to live. They can only tell you how to re-create the life they currently are living. It is time to rely on information from people who enjoy the type of relationships you would like to have; who have the type of professional lifestyle and personal life that you want to enjoy. My married friends and I all have had great professional success in our lives, and we all have been happily married for an average of more than twenty years.

Prepare yourself to embark on a special journey of discovery. I will show you how to unlock the keys to finding that special someone. I will show where you are most likely to meet the type of person you are seeking. First, you have to believe that you can be happy and that you deserve to be happy. It doesn't matter which faith you believe in; they all have one thing in common—that there is a higher power that wants you to have a great life, be happy, and have someone special to share it with. When you believe this, the stage is set.

Throughout this book I will discuss what it takes to be successful in your personal life. I will talk about how to use self-assessment techniques to determine what is working for you and what is not. Then I will show you how to develop the skills necessary to be as successful in your personal relationships as you have been in your professional life. My advice is supplemented by a number of true stories to demonstrate particular points. These stories are highlighted inside gray text boxes; the names of the people mentioned in these stories have been changed to protect their identities.

You have already begun your journey to achieving greater success in your personal life by selecting this book. You now have the opportunity to discover another way to achieve and enhance your happiness. I will not promise it is going to be easy, but I can promise you will have fun throughout the process, and if you need more personal one-on-one assistance, I'll even show you the best places and people to go to for excellent help, advice, and service. Let's get started on changing your life.

CHAPTER 1

Attraction – How to Attract the Right One

Let's face it: it's not easy to know what might attract another person. But once you understand what men and women are looking for, you'll easily be able to tell if you can attract the type of person with whom you want to spend your life.

DO A SELF-ASSESSMENT

Physical attraction is a powerful lure for most human beings. It's the thing that sparks our interest when someone catches our eye and makes us think, "Hey, I would like to meet that person!" But what does it mean to be physically attractive *and* physically attracted to someone? Initially, the way you look at someone can be a powerful tool. Simply smiling at him or her (regardless of how you perceive your own physical attractiveness) can be effective and is a great way to show your personality. Your clothes, your style, and how you carry yourself also reveal a lot about you. All of these can be used to communicate your interest in someone and attract favorable attention.

How confident is your smile? If it lacks confidence, start working on improving and practicing your smile, as well as fixing any dental issues. And what about your personality? Does it say, "Hey, I am fun, exciting, and open to meeting you"? Or does it say, "Stay away!" because you looked away just at the moment someone tried to make a connection? People look for signals that tell them whether or not it's safe to approach someone. Therefore, it's important to be aware of what you are communicating to people—verbally and especially non-verbally. As you search for the perfect partner, learn how to use your eyes, smile, and personality, effectively and confidently, to attract that someone. You never know—that guy who glanced at you and smiled briefly may be the man you have been looking for all your life. Or the beautiful lady who gave you a cute smile could be your soul mate. Master your alluring but innocent look, and be open to the possibilities a new connection could bring. It is okay to appear approachable while maintaining your inner strength—this applies to both men and women.

Many professionals have a hard time differentiating between their professional and personal clothing. They tend to blend the two into one and then wonder why no one looks up when they walk into the room. Men and women like to see each other well dressed and well groomed and dressed appropriate to the occasion. Your clothes and accessories communicate a great deal about you as a person. If you wear the same outfits for both your work and personal life, it may communicate to a potential partner that you are all work and no play. It may also communicate that you might not know how to unwind or that you did not think to go home and change into something more appropriate for the occasion or venue. You always want to look your best, no matter where you are—people do notice.

I think we can all agree that true beauty is in the details. No matter what height, shape, or size you are, you can still accentuate the positive things about your appearance. Get your hair styled, and practice good hygiene. Simple things like clipping, shaping, and cleaning under your nails shows you care about the way you look. Taking the time to clean and polish your shoes and making sure they are in good repair illustrates you care about the little things too. New shoes always make a great statement, providing you have good taste in your selection. I offer suggestions about what constitutes good taste in chapter 8, "Dressing to Impress." I think wearing an appropriate, proportional outfit that accentuates your best features tastefully can make a bold statement. Also wearing a *small* amount of cologne or perfume with a subtle, pleasant scent rarely goes unnoticed. When you wear too much, it is overpowering and completely gives the wrong impression. How you carry yourself says the most about you. Be careful that you leave your work persona at work and let your personal persona make your statement in your private life—it's important to differentiate between the two. This concept seems to be the hardest thing for many professional, career-minded people to grasp. If you find this to be true in your life, you've identified the first issue you need to work on.

Every day I hear men and women talk about losing weight and getting back into the gym. It's a great idea to keep yourself toned and in shape, but that doesn't mean you need to develop and maintain the body of a cheerleader or quarterback. For a moment, think about men's expectations and women's expectations for a mate. Most men like women with good figures, and most women like men with good physiques. What defines a good figure or a good physique varies widely from person to person. There is no true ideal, even though commercial television and the fashion industry would like all of us to think so. The truth is that different people like different things—that will never change. There are some things, however, that I hope we can agree on. If you've completed your self-assessment and believe you have addressed all the suggested areas, then it's time to go on to the next evaluation. You must know what people are looking for in a potential partner.

WHAT DO MEN LOOK FOR?

Some men do not mind if a woman has a little extra padding; some prefer very thin women. In my experience, however, I've found that most men agree they would prefer a woman who is toned and shapely, no matter what size she is. I often recommend to my female clients who struggle with weight issues to focus on toning themselves and developing a waistline. Ladies, I recommend you worry less about the pounds and focus more on your overall look. You will rarely, if ever, hear a man say that a woman's rear end or chest is too big. Just focus on creating definition between the two.

Sadly, many men rely on visual attraction. When most men first see a woman, they usually check out her face, her bust, her butt, and her legs. Men are very simple creatures. In my observations and discussions with men all over the world, physical appearance carries a lot of weight with many of them. However, their definition of what constitutes good looks varies widely. One man may find a woman very beautiful, while another may not appreciate her particular look. It comes down to personal taste. That is why I believe there is somebody out there for everyone. The old saying "Beauty is in the eye of the beholder" is still true.

A lot of women ask me, "Why don't more men appreciate smart, successful, hard-working women?" I have to say they do—there may not be enough of them today, but they are out there. I believe, though, that even these men put a great deal of importance on how fun the woman is to be with. These men will appreciate a woman's accomplishments and her professional status, but they also will want the softer side of her when she comes home. Women need to turn off their work persona and turn on their personal persona when they spend time with their men and their family. This also applies to men when they come home to their women and families. It's hard but highly recommended.

Men tend to look for very simple qualities when they initially select a partner, but these carry a lot of importance. I find the following traits and qualities to be consistent considerations for most men that I have met:

1. Is she attractive? (Definition varies widely)
2. Is she sexy? (Definition varies widely)
3. Is she fun to be with (e.g., good company, good conversationalist, exciting, intriguing)?
4. Does she have a nice body? (Definition varies widely)
5. Will she be a good sex partner? (Definition varies widely)
6. Is she a nice person? (Does she have a great attitude and a good personality?)

7. Can she hold her own in any environment (e.g., with my friends, family, colleagues)? Does she adapt quickly to environments and situations and make the most of them?

I call these the 7 Points of Attraction. It doesn't mean that other things are not important, because they are. It means that a lot of men base their initial decision about women on their physical and social attributes, and *then they dig deeper into who she really is and what is she about*. The woman who meets most of his desired traits has the best chance of capturing his heart and becoming part of his life.

I always tell my female friends and clients to down-play their career success at first. Some women have lucrative careers and high-powered positions. Some men may be intimidated by a woman's success initially and see her as someone they need to compete with and impress, rather than someone they want to date and build a relationship with. This is sad but oftentimes true. So when men want to know what you do for a living, instead of saying "I'm a CFO, (vice president, COO, or doctor)," consider saying, "I'm in finance (or management, or in business operations, or in healthcare)." Then refocus the conversation back to him. You want to discover what you two have in common, not discuss your professional life. It's too soon. Keep him interested in the personal side of your life. I know you are really proud of your achievements and so am I. But that conversation is not one you want to have with your date at this point. Show him what makes you so exciting and intriguing to be with.

WHAT DO WOMEN LOOK FOR?

Most women tend to look for much more than a man's looks, physique, and sex appeal. Women like attractive, sexy men (definition varies widely) who are intriguing and can pique their interest as well. They like their men to be clean-cut and well groomed. Women like a man who dresses to impress—not flashy but fashionable. Women like to ask their girlfriends what they think of a man, and those friends' first impressions will be based on how you look and carry yourself. So short or tall, skinny or big-boned, men should always dress to impress and bring their "A game." But more importantly, *women want to know if a man is accomplished, career-minded, and upwardly mobile (i.e., working to get ahead).* They also look for substance, like:

- Does he have a job?
- Does he have a great personality? (Definition varies widely)
- Will he treat me well?
- Will I have **fun** with him?
- Is he exciting?
- Is he honest, trustworthy, and responsible?
- Will my family like him?
- Is he nurturing?
- Will he be a good sex partner?
- Will he make a good husband and father?
- Does he carry himself well?
- Can he hold his own in any environment?
- Is he confident but not arrogant or too sure of himself?
- Is he a good person or a bad boy?

Ladies tend to be more interested in how a man approaches her and how he will treat her for the long term. The bottom line is *women are looking for substance*, not witty pickup lines or a lot of flash. They cut right through a man's fancy pickup lines and begin to evaluate whether he is someone they should take seriously—or dismiss politely. They want to know who you really are as a person. If you find that just being yourself is not achieving the right results, get a life coach or relationship coach to help you improve the areas you need to work on. For instance, most men could benefit from a little extra work in learning how best to approach women. If men are serious about attracting the best women, they will have to consider how well they stack up against her expectations of a man and adjust accordingly. I do not believe any of the criteria I listed is too much to expect of any man.

KNOW WHAT YOU ARE LOOKING FOR

Many people are unsuccessful in finding the "right partner" because they do not know what they are looking for in a partner. They have not spent enough time clearly defining what traits, characteristics, or features they prefer their future partner to have. Equally—if not more importantly—people also need to decide which traits they do *not* want in a potential partner. Let me introduce you to my friend Michael, who found himself frustrated and wondering about his future and finding the right person.

Michael had just completed graduate school in Texas. He was handsome, smart, well dressed, and equipped with a master's degree in hospital administration from one of Texas's most prestigious universities and a new high-paying job in Tulsa, Oklahoma. One night not long after graduation, Michael found himself with his old college buddies in a local bar, enjoying a night of drinks and hoping to find a great woman to be with.

After Michael surveyed the bar scene, he quickly realized this could end up being his daily personal life going forward. He had already achieved great scholastic and initial career success but found his life lacking in the personal area. He started talking to himself, saying, "Am I going to spend the rest of my life looking at barflies, hoping to find the right woman to complete my life and raise a family with?" Michael suddenly became depressed and quickly realized he was going to have to put some serious time into his personal life if he was going to escape the life of a single professional who cruised the bars nightly, looking for someone special. He knew he needed to sit down and determine exactly what he was looking for in a woman and where best to find her.

He did not want just anyone; he wanted someone special to love and spend the rest of his life with. Michael knew he wasn't about to find that kind of woman in the bars he and his friends frequented. Michael identified the traits and qualities that were important to him and ended up getting back together with his college sweetheart. He realized that she had everything he was looking for. He married her after recognizing she would complete his dreams, love him faithfully, enhance his life, and build the family he imagined.

The moral of this story is quite simple: Michael took the time to discover what he *didn't* want, which made it much easier to determine what he *did* want in a partner—and then he could make the right decision in his selection.

So many people make the mistake of trying to find the right partner before they determine what they are really looking for. You have to start by doing a little homework—nothing too difficult or time-consuming but something that will improve your search and selection efforts by at least tenfold. With that kind of increase in your chances for success, isn't it worth doing a little up-front work? You do it all the time in your job, so why not do it in your personal life as well?

First, take an introspective look at yourself and then an outward look, and assess who you really are. You should assess what is good about you, what could be improved, and what you have to offer a potential partner. This will answer the question, "Am I a good catch?" I strongly encourage you to turn to your family and closest friends and ask them to be truly honest with you with their feedback. Some of it may be hard to hear, but it's *essential* if you really want to make a change in your personal life. Please be open to their comments and suggestions. They have your best interest at heart, and it's really hard to tell people things they need to improve. Remember, you cannot improve something unless you are aware of it.

Next, I believe it will be very beneficial to ask the same team of people to help you identify and clarify your important considerations when choosing a potential partner. You can bounce ideas off your "team," as well as have them point out when you are not being realistic about your expectations. If nothing else, they can ask you the following questions and record your answers for you to review later. You might want to consider things like:

- How important is physical attraction?
- What features are important?
  - Physique, shape, height, weight, eye color, hairstyle and color, facial hair or no facial hair, bald, etc.

- How do you feel about the way the person dresses?
- Do you like tattoos, body or facial piercing?
- What is your favorite look (e.g., conservative, edgy, sexy, casual, grunge, country-western, rugged, bad boy, nerdy)?
- How important are race, age, culture, background, social class, and religion?
- How important are good physical and financial health?
- How important are educational achievement, type of job, and career or profession?
- How important is location?
  - Would you consider dating someone long distance?
  - Would you relocate for the right partner?
- What common interests would you like for your potential partner to share?
  - ***This is a very critical question!*** *Many relationships fail when people grow apart because they do not like to do the same things. They do not have enough shared interests.*
- How important are personality traits?
  - What type of personality are you looking for?
  - Will it complement or conflict with your personality?
- How do you feel about romance, sex, travel, family, children, his or her friends, family, pets, etc.?
- Would you ever consider expanding your pool of potential partners by dating interracially, inter-culturally, inter-religiously, or with someone from another country or area?

These are extremely tough questions to consider, and you need to be honest. The more truthful your answers are, the more successful your search and selection of the right partner will be. Keep your expectations realistic! Let me introduce you to my sister's criteria.

> *My sister always said she wanted to date and marry a handsome black surgeon who played golf and owned a boat. I have been telling her for years that the number of single professional men in the world who fit that description is extremely small.*
>
> *This ultimately means that unless she widens her selection criteria, it will be very hard for her to find the right man.*

The moral of this story is the more things you ask for in a potential partner, the shorter your list of likely candidates becomes.

There is probably no such thing as a "perfect partner," but knowing in advance what type of person would make you happy definitely improves your chances of finding someone close to perfect for you. You may not snag the next Angelina Jolie, or Brad Pitt, or Denzel Washington, or Halle Berry, or Selma Hayek, or Antonio Banderas, or Eva Mendes, or Antonio Sabato, or Carrie Underwood, or Blake Shelton, but you can snag the right partner for you. He or she is definitely out there—you can count on it—but you have to have realistic expectations.

Now that you know what you want and do not want from a partner, we need to work on a few things. But first, I want you to reiterate that the more things you ask for in a potential partner the harder it will be to find someone that fits your criteria. Figure out what's most important to you and be open to someone that fits most of your criteria. Too many people ask for too much and seek partners that are not realistic. If you remain open there are endless possibilities for you to choose from. The next topic focuses on recommended changes you might want to consider, as well as how to develop the skills to attract the right person.

CONSIDER GETTING A MAKEOVER

Changing your look can increase the attention you attract when you walk into a room—in a good way! This applies to both men and women. If your look and your current wardrobe do not make the impression you expected, why not consider making a change? What do you have to lose? A makeover can be as subtle or as extensive as you want. For some of you, subtle tweaks will make all the difference in the world. For others, a complete makeover may be the right prescription to give you a fresh start. But for most people, a few subtle changes in appearance can really rev up your personal life, especially if you feel good about the change. Once you feel good about yourself, that feeling actually comes out in your eyes, your smile, and your personality. Please remember these are very powerful weapons for attraction when used correctly.

Some people are concerned about doing a makeover. They may be concerned that the final result will be a façade that does not reflect their true personality. The most important thing to remember is to accentuate your best attributes. You could receive a radical makeover or do something as simple as changing the style, length, or color of your hair—tastefully, of course! It also might involve buying a new outfit or updating your wardrobe. Just think of the fun you will have shopping. And if you do not like shopping for new clothes and accessories, consider using a personal shopper or a makeover specialist to assist in creating the "new" you. Many department stores have personal shopper services—some provide it for a fee and some for free. A specialist will work with you to put together your best overall look. This is available for both men and women. As a professional/career-minded person, you know the importance of looking your best and the need to invest in your future. The type of outfits that will impress your boss and colleagues at work, however, may not be the right ones to impress that someone special you may run into after work, or over the weekend, or while shopping, or while on vacation. It is critically important that you learn to dress for the occasion.

People frequently ask, "Where is the best place to find nice singles?" I respond, "Why don't you go to the grocery store in your neighborhood?" You would be surprised how many great single people there are at the local grocery store. You can even practice your smile and eye contact and your ability to talk to people you do not know. Please remember you need to look well groomed and dressed nicely, even in casual wear. Your old, rumpled clothes will rarely make a good impression. Consider updating them with something appealing, casual, and comfortable. People always notice what you are wearing and what you look like. If you don't know what's appealing, please take someone with good fashion sense shopping with you. Also please remember to brush your hair and freshen your breath before you go to the store. That special person you have been searching and hoping for might be standing at the deli counter right next to you, checking you out. Always be prepared to make the right impression. Smile and simply say, "Hi, how are you to-day? What do you like best from this deli?" And let the conversation flow from there.

More subtle changes could involve buying new shoes or changing your style of shoes. This is particularly relevant for men who tend to put less importance on their shoes. Shoes, however, are one of the first things women look at when they check out men. If you are not sure what to buy or what is in style, take one of your style-conscious friends to help advise you. I always take a woman with me to help me pick out clothes, shoes, eyeglasses, and accessories. Women know what they like to see on a man, and men know what they like to see on a woman. (There's nothing like watching a woman walk down the street wearing a beautifully styled pair of shoes that complements a well-fitted outfit.)

No matter what you decide to buy, you still have to dress for the occasion. Not many women are impressed by a man's wearing tennis shoes or flip-flops with a dressy outfit or if he looks like he just fell out of bed. For men with facial hair, trimming your beard or mustache or actually shaving it off and sporting a clean-cut look could be a great change of pace and a way to attract more positive attention.

For women, particularly professional/career-mined women, changing your makeup or starting to wear a little makeup can really get you noticed, not only in your private life but also in your business life. You may want to think about accentuating the features that people are normally attracted to—your eyes, your lips, and your cheekbones. Select makeup that complements your skin tone, use just enough to highlight your best features, and be sure your style is up-to-date. I personally believe that the single greatest "return on investment" for both men and women is to lose some weight or tone their bodies. It does more than just get you noticed; it also makes you feel good about yourself—and that radiates to everyone with whom you come in contact. You'll start to walk a little differently, sit a little differently, and wear your clothes a little differently. You don't have to become model-thin or toned like a body builder, just tone your body to the point where you feel physically and mentally healthier. That does not equate to a specific dress or pants size but to a look that says to all, "I feel good about myself, and I hope you appreciate all the work I have put into looking good."

Think of the possibilities if you joined a co-ed fitness center; you never know who you might meet while getting healthier. If going to a fitness center is out of the question, consider walking or biking a few miles several times a week with a friend. Before you know it, you will start receiving those positive comments followed by the right type of attention from people.

You can easily change your diet by simply adding something new and healthful each week while taking away something less nutritious. This will deliver significant improvement to your overall body, health, and look. Remember, when someone is looking for a long-term partner and relationship, he or she wants someone who looks like he or she is going to be around for a long time to share those special times together. Good health and a good body are definitely important components for you to seriously consider and work on as part of your personal makeover strategy.

Dressing for success is often applied to business environments, but it applies equally well to your personal life.

Let me introduce you to my friend Shelly, and you'll see how this simple concept changed her life.

My friend Shelly is a very successful up-and-coming corporate manager. She is attractive, extremely smart, has great personality, and is a go-getter! However, Shelly found herself stuck at the manager level when she desperately wanted to be a director and perhaps a corporate vice president one day. She also was very lonely because she basically dedicated her entire life to her career and her son—she was a single mom. One day Shelly came to me and said, "Charles, how do I get promoted? I keep watching the guys move ahead, and I know I am as good if not better at my job than many of them. Also, I really would like to balance my life and maintain a good work/life balance that includes a husband who loves me and my son."

I looked at her and said, "First we have to change you. You need to learn to look the part before you get the part. You have to learn to fake it until you make it." I sat down with her and helped her assess herself, both professionally and personally. I recommended that she needed to wear a little conservative makeup and more business outfits. Shelly had joined the company as soon as she graduated from the University of California, Berkeley, at age twenty-one. Even though she had facilitated and integrated over fifty national and global company acquisitions, many still saw her as the cute young girl we'd hired straight out of school, based on the way she dressed. We had to change her image so that staff and clients would take her role more seriously.

Shelly started wearing her long curly hair down instead of her usual bun or French-roll style, and she applied very conservative makeup that highlighted her best features. I sent her shopping to buy conservative yet fashionable business suits and dresses for work.

Once she pieced it all together and began to sport her new look at work, her whole life changed. Executives started to take notice of her and her new grown-up appearance. They talked about her future and plans for giving her increased responsibility. She started getting invited to more corporate-level meetings. She received her promotion within two months of making the transformation.

Shelly also applied the same advice to her personal life. Her dating calendar picked up, guys started to notice her more, and she received some very complimentary comments about her appearance and overall appeal to those men.

With just a few minor changes to her look, Shelly was able to transform her life and her career. It turned out to be a life-changing experience.

The same makeover approach works for guys too. Simple things—such as not wearing white socks with black pants and shoes; not wearing T-shirts that are stained or have holes in them—are easy to change. I believe wearing clean, well-fitting, complementary-colored clothes and accessories dramatically increases a man's attractiveness. My belief is based on feedback from hundreds of women worldwide about what they like to see in a man.

Are you ready for your makeover?

SUMMARY

There is someone out there for everyone. You just have to believe in yourself and believe that you deserve someone. Many things help attract attention, but the most critical are your eyes (the way you look at someone), your smile, and your personality. Do an assessment of yourself and know what you have to offer and what your best assets are. Men tend to put a lot of emphasis on physical attraction initially, but their opinions on what makes a woman physically attractive varies widely. Women like attractive men as well, but they put more emphasis on what kind of man is he. Women like substance!

Know what you are looking for in a partner. Take the time to figure out what's important to you. You want to develop the makeup of your ideal partner. Once you complete that, you will find that it is much easier to recognize the type of person you are looking for. Make sure your expectations are realistic. Some people look for so many things in a partner that even God has not figured out how to make that kind of individual. Please make sure you are looking for the type of person that really does exist on earth.

If there is something about your appearance that you would like to change—change it! I'm not a big believer in plastic surgery. I believe in accentuating the things you already have to work with. A simple makeover can do wonders for most people and increase their appeal substantially. Ask your closest friend and family members for suggestions, or tell them what you are considering changing and get their feedback. Once your makeover is complete, you are well on your way to creating the "new you."

CHAPTER 2

Change Your Routine

Let's look at your activity calendar. I want you to seriously consider doing activities that are new and different from your normal routine. You need to break your old routines, even if it causes you to spend less time with some of your current friends. Why? Because many people believe they can keep on doing the same things over and over again and get different results. My experience observing many people trying this approach only showed me that, unfortunately, they just kept getting more of the same results.

If you do not make a change in your life, you will continue to be frustrated, and nothing will change unless you make that first step outside of your box. Please consider taking a step outside of your normal comfort zone. Perhaps you want to take up golf or tennis; go bowling; attend ball games, concerts, art exhibits, comedy clubs, live poetry events, or activities in your local parks; or go to outdoor cafes or wine bars. You can start to pick up or attend an unlimited number of activities that will introduce you to a new circle of friends and increase significantly your potentially meeting someone special. And if nothing else, you will start to meet more people who like the same type of activities as you do. Remember, one of the keys to relationship compatibility is finding someone who likes to do the same types of things you like to enjoy. Why not consider participating in activities that attract the type of person you like? It can open you up to a wealth of new friends, exciting activities, and potential partners. I can assure you that Mr. or Miss Right is not going to come knocking on your door! You have to get out and about; you won't find him or her if you stay snuggled up on the sofa with a good book or watching TV.

I believe everyone should travel often—and globally. Nothing excites me more than traveling to a new and exciting place, meeting new people, and experiencing new things. I recently went to Paris with my wife, Pauline, and we could not believe how many people of different cultures, ethnicities, and religions we saw dating or just hanging out together in widely diverse groups. It made us think of our clients, and we wondered just how many opportunities each of them would have if they opened themselves up to all the possibilities and prospects available in the world. It would be a beautiful thing to see!

You never know who you might meet while traveling or vacationing—or where it all can lead. For me, it led to finding and marrying a beautiful English girl and raising a family of four beautiful girls. We found each other in Greece and married six months later. We have been married thirty-two years.

Think about traveling to increase your exposure to myriad possibilities. And yes, you can go traveling on your own, particularly when you go with tour groups. Just be sure to let someone close to you know your itinerary, advise him or her of any changes, and check in with that person regularly during your trip.

PROPS

It is very easy to attract the right kind of attention if you use a prop. Actors, actresses, circus performers, and entertainers who seek to capture and hold our attention throughout their performances have mastered the technique of using props. You can use the same concept to capture the attention of other people. The following are a few examples; find one you can identify with and put it to work.

Walking the Dog

The first rule in using a prop is that your prop must be able to attract attention tastefully and compel someone (the right someone) to approach you. Consider getting a cute dog or borrowing one from a friend—a dog that attracts people and won't frighten them. Consider friendly dogs like golden retrievers, schnauzers, pugs, cocker spaniels, springer spaniels, Yorkshire terriers, huskies, Labradors, or collies. There are so many breeds of friendly dogs to choose from.

Next step: walk your dog in areas like parks, sidewalk café areas, outdoor shopping areas, around the neighborhood, around your condo or apartment building, at PetSmart, etc. You will be surprised by how many people will approach you because they want to talk about your dog.

Remember, though, it's important to have a friendly dog. Women and men both will approach someone if the pet does not scare them or display aggression. They often will ask if they can pet your dog, and they'll ask your dog's name or what type of dog it is. They want to know how long you have had the dog or where you got him. They also might ask you if your dog is a good dog and if you often walk around the area. Now the important point to remember is the dog is your prop as well as your trusted friend, but do not forget to make and keep eye contact as you interact with your admirer. Who knows? He or she might like you as well as your dog.

A benefit of using the dog as a prop is that if you do not like the people who approach you, you still have your dog at your side to help keep you safe. Now let's take the conversation and interaction to the next level.

When someone you are attracted to approaches you to talk about your dog, *use your common interest in dogs as an icebreaker*. Ask the person if he or she has a dog. Ask what kind of dog it is and what the dog's name is. Ask her if she walks her dog in this area as well or where she prefers to walk her dog. Tell him which special areas you have found for walking your dog. You also can talk about choice of veterinarians or dog-sitters.

Any of these questions will open up the conversation and allow you to have an interaction about dogs. You may be able to leverage this meeting to ask the person if he or she would like your two dogs to walk or play together. Many dog owners like to arrange play dates for their pets. But take it slow, and please do not be pushy! If you are classy and allow your personality to show and remain at ease with your conversation, good things should develop.

You two already have something in common—your pets. Now, remember to follow through. It can be something as simple as saying, "I always walk my dog around this time. I hope to see you again." Or "I would love for our two dogs to meet. I would love for my dog to have another dog to play with sometimes." The person will pick up on both your direct and indirect meanings. This is a great approach for men to use, but don't be pushy! Let it evolve.

Kid in the Stroller

Have you ever noticed how a cute kid in a stroller attracts women? Take your sister's, brother's, or friend's child—or your kid—for a walk in the stroller. Children are a great way to attract attention, particularly if they are adorable and well behaved. I have found that when men push a stroller, women will often approach them to ask about the kid. They will ask you if the baby is yours, or they'll be impressed if you are babysitting someone else's child. They will tell you how cute the child is, and ask you the child's name and age.

Remember, this is your mutual common interest. Be sure to make eye contact, and don't look down at the ground or away when you are talking—this shows a lack of confidence. Give her your best smile. Take your time; do not feel like you have to rush. Smoothly guide the conversation to focus more on her. You can ask her if she likes children. Does she have any children? What are their ages? Depending on how well your conversation is going, you can consider asking her if she is married. If she is, thank her for her kind comments and move on. If she is not and you feel attracted to her, continue talking to her about the child and say that you are glad you bumped into each other.

You may want to consider asking her to walk along with you. Try to maintain a connection that puts her at ease, and keep your conversation on common ground. You might ask her what she likes to do or if she knows of any cool places or upcoming events in the area. But whatever you do, do not get too pushy, or you will alarm her. Also, please do not forget you have a child with you. *Be attentive to the child's needs first*, or your conversation will be cut short quickly by an unhappy, screaming, or whining child.

So consider walking the kid in areas where women frequent, like malls, public parks, shopping areas, condo- or apartment-based areas, etc. You can also attract attention by taking the child to the playground. There are always single moms, dads, and relatives at neighborhood playgrounds where you can easily initiate a conversation. The swings are great places to meet and interact with someone.

TAKE A DANCE CLASS

The hottest activity sweeping the nation right now is Latin and ballroom dancing. Spurred on by popular shows like *So You Think You Can Dance* and *Dancing with the Stars*, Latin and ballroom dancing have reached mainstream America. Thousands of Latin music clubs have opened up over the last few years across the country, attracting crowds of beautiful people in sexy outfits, ready to demonstrate their best sexy moves on the dance floor. Guys, if you have never seen a woman shaking her hips in a Latin dance, or elegantly floating across the floor in a ballroom dance, or witnessed or been a part of a country line dance, you have missed a real treat. Ladies, if you have never seen a man rhythmically glide across the floor, moving his feet and body to the rhythms and sexy beats of rumba, merengue, salsa, fox trot, jive, waltz, or two-step, you have missed out.

If you lack the knowledge to dance to Latin, ballroom, or country music or lack confidence in your dancing ability, don't worry. There are many like you. Go take dance lessons. There are dance studios practically in every town and city across the nation. Dance studios are one of the best places to meet new people who have some of the same interests as you do. Anyone can learn to dance. You may never dance like Cheryl Burke or Maks Chmerkovskiy from *Dancing with the Stars*, but you can certainly learn to dance well enough to attract the attention of new friends and potential partners.

First step: look up dance lessons in your local area and find a studio that meets your needs. Arthur Murray and Fred Astaire Dance Studios are well known nationwide and offer both Latin and ballroom classes, from beginners to competition-level dancers.

The nice thing about Latin and ballroom dancing is they both require a partner. If you do not have a partner to bring with you to the studio, they will pair you up with one once you get there. That makes it all the more fun, because when you make mistakes you are making them in front of someone who is also trying not to make mistakes. Your fretting over your mistakes can turn into an interesting conversation starter between you and a potential new friend or partner. Remember, you are both learning at the same time and mistakes are natural and part of the learning process. Don't be afraid to laugh at yourself and enjoy the process of learning together.

LADIES: Take a look around the studio at all the available men, but please do not base your decision on outward appearance only. You could be eliminating a wonderful person without ever giving him a chance. Remember, looks fade over time, but having someone who is fun and has a good personality, mutual interests, and a caring nature, and is trustworthy will endure.

Watch the way the men take instruction, the way they rehearse and practice, and how they observe others in the class. Pay attention to the way they move, their energy, and their confidence level. You can learn a great deal about a person just by observing him and how he interacts with others.

You will probably have rotating partners throughout the class, but you may also have the opportunity to select a partner—at least at the beginning. You will want to be in close proximity to the one you have your eye on because if you like him, someone else probably does as well. Select or rotate to your preferred partner when you get the chance. Say hello and introduce yourself by simply saying, "My name is ____" and then ask his name. Remember, your energy level, smile, and eyes are key. Your voice should be warm and polite. You should sound happy to be there and that you enjoy dancing. It is okay to be nervous because he is probably as nervous as you. This type of dance is something new to both of you. Call him by name periodically while you are dancing and talking together. Keeping your eye contact is paramount, but be subtle—don't stare. You might want to say something that puts him at ease. He needs to understand that there's no pressure for him to be the perfect dance partner.

Consider something like, "I may not be a great dancer, but it sure is fun trying to learn." Or "I have always loved dancing. Just moving makes me feel so alive." Or "If we can keep the beat and move our feet, we are halfway there. Learning these new steps and moves is part of the fun."

These types of comments will put him more at ease and increase his comfort level.

You may want to consider complimenting him on something that struck you about him while you were checking him out before class started. Giving him a compliment he would not expect can help break the ice. You could say something like: "You look very sharp in that suit"; "That shirt is a great color on you"; "I like your strong hands. The way you hold me gives me a lot of confidence that you will be there for me as we master these moves"; "I like your smile"; "I see you like to practice. So do I"; "One day you will be the best dancer in our class"; and so on. Any of these comments will break the ice and put him at ease; if not, move on to someone new and interesting.

When the class is nearly over, thank him for dancing with you, and tell him you enjoyed dancing together. Tell him you hope to partner with him again, or suggest that you are very open to meeting before the next class to practice. Most dance studios have a room where you can practice either before or after class. If you are really interested in him and feel the chemistry between you, ask him to meet you for practice and set a firm date and time. Remember, it is really easy to break the ice when you have something in common with someone. What better icebreaker is there than dancing as partners? Good luck!

MEN: The above scenario is focused on women, but guys, you can see how you can easily turn it around and apply the same questions, recommendations, and approaches to a woman who interests you in your dance class. Women are mostly thinking the same things as you are, except the majority of them will not approach you. Put them at ease and make the first move to introduce yourself. Despite what you may think or have been told, most women like a potential partner to initiate the first move. Be poised. Don't be shy. Women absolutely love a man who can dance.

ATTEND A WEDDING

You just received another invitation to attend a friend's wedding. But instead of getting anxious and wondering how could you get out of it without hurting his or her feelings and your relationship, consider a different viewpoint. *Weddings can be a high-quality singles event.* Weddings are great events to meet other single people who may be looking for the same thing you are looking for—something real, something permanent, and something special. Everyone knows weddings tend to be very joyous and happy occasions. Love is in the air, and everyone is more open to talking, dancing, and having a good time than during many other social events. Typically, there is good food, great drinks, and lots of dancing.

Now, think back to those dance lessons you just completed. You now have the perfect opportunity to show off your new moves and confidence. Weddings are the perfect setup for encouraging couples to dance closely together in honor of the bride and groom. And if that does not work for you, just wait until the dance music starts so you can show your new stuff. Nothing is more impressive than watching a man and woman who can dance well, especially latin or ballroom dance. It is so sexy and fun. Ladies love men who can line dance. So learn a couple great line-dance routines, and be ready to strut your stuff.

This upcoming wedding could be a great opportunity to meet new people and perhaps that special someone, so it is critical that you prepare in advance. Ask the lucky bride and groom about the single people who will be attending their wedding. You know they have someone in mind for you already. They may be able to introduce you to someone special or sit you at the same table. Plan to attend by yourself or with friends and see what opportunities unfold. It is okay not to bring a date and to hang out with your friends or just concentrate on meeting someone new and exciting once you get there.

Dress to impress: This is one of the few opportunities to wear your best classy outfit, but please do not upstage the bride or groom. You should consider wearing something you love that truly highlights your best features. It may even be sexy but should be subtle, tasteful, and classy.

Once you are at the wedding, observe people entering the church or venue and during the wedding, and mingle after the wedding. You may see someone you are interested in meeting and learning more about. If possible, determine if that person is single. Ask the bridesmaids or groomsmen if they know the person and if they would introduce you. And if not, be bold and introduce yourself. All it takes is a simple hi and tell the person your name. You might ask, "Are you enjoying the celebration?" or even just ask his or her name. Tell the person how you know the bride and groom, and ask how he or she knows them. Remember to talk about things you have in common; in this case, it is the friendship with the bride and/or groom or whichever of their close friends that invited you. Ask the person if he or she is going to the reception, and say you look forward to seeing him or her there.

If the reception is within walking distance and the initial chemistry seems to be there, ask if he or she would like to walk together to the reception. If the reception is driving distance, say, "I hope to see you there," deliver a friendly handshake, and give your best smile before you walk away. It is important that you show a little of your magic in your handshake and through your eyes. I would gently take a woman's hand and softly squeeze it before turning her hand over and softly kissing the back of her hand. Chivalry is not dead, and women simply love it—it makes them feel special. And ladies, it is okay to give his hand a little squeeze, accompanied by your best smile and alluring eyes, just to let him know you think he might be something special. Do not forget to always keep your lipstick fresh. And everyone should carry and use breath mints or sprays. Be natural and relax.

Once you arrive at the reception, if you still haven't met anyone of interest, start to mingle and casually talk to people. Just be friendly and use your smile and eyes to work the room. If you do not know how to use your smile and eyes effectively, just take notice of someone who does and mimic that behavior.

If the bride or groom previously agreed to introduce you to someone, try to find out who it is and introduce yourself. They have too many others things going on. You can always introduce yourself by saying that your friend (the bride or groom) wanted to make sure you two met. You must have something in common or your friend would never have suggested that you two meet. So take the chance and introduce yourself.

LADIES: If there is not assigned seating at the reception, wait to see where the person you are interested in is sitting, stand behind a chair at his table, and ask him if he minds if you sit there. I do not think he will object. You want to establish eye contact immediately with your best smile and introduce yourself. It is important to be natural, happy, and charismatic. People tend to open up more to people who are genuine, happy, and charismatic—but not over-the-top enthusiastic. Say hello or hi and tell him your name. Be sure to radiate confidence by maintaining your eye contact and extending your hand in friendship. Ask his name, if he hasn't already told you. Take the time to repeat his name and say that you are pleased to meet him (for example, "Hi. I'm pleased to meet you, Jim.") This will help you remember his name, ensure you have heard his name correctly, and make your following conversation more personal. Consider offering a sincere compliment about the person's outfit, hair, smile, eyes, shoes, accessories, etc. I usually recommend that you do not say how beautiful or handsome she or he is, even if the person is breathtaking. Say something original that highlights the subtle things about the person. People go to great lengths to highlight their best features or select that eye-catching outfit or suit. A compliment about it will be well received.

MEN: Once you have made your initial contact and exchanged introductions, it is time to enter the discovery phase. Ask her how long she has known the bride and/or groom. Ask her if she has any special memories of them. Ask her what she thought of the wedding ceremony. When it is time to toast the bride and groom, touch your glasses together as you toast.

When it is time to dance, ask her to dance with you and hold her hand lightly while escorting her to the dance floor. It is okay to tastefully touch her hand or shoulder while dancing, if you feel the chemistry is there between you. But please, always be polite and respectful. All of these things will lay the path for a great evening and a possible future date.

LADIES: Please let him know you are interested. Give him a special smile as you toast to the bride and groom. Hold his hand as he escorts you to the dance floor. Flirt a little as you dance with him, but keep your composure. Squeeze his hand and thank him for the dance as you walk back to your table.

MEN: If you are hitting it off and have good chemistry, continue your conversation once you return to the table. Flirt a little, but be tasteful and classy. Ask more questions about her to see what other interests you have in common, like dancing, movies, concerts, etc. Ask questions like, "Where is your favorite place to go? Do you like to travel? Do you like the theater? Do you enjoy art exhibits or visiting museums? Are you a sports fan? What are your favorite sports and teams?" Ask her if she has ever attended a game and if she enjoyed it. These are all simple ways to discover what interests you have in common. Keep the conversation focused on her and limit your comments about you to just enough to keep her interested.

LADIES: If you are sure the chemistry is there; offer him your card with your e-mail address on it and perhaps your phone number, and see if he reciprocates by offering his. If not, nothing lost. You still had a great time. If you do not have a card, you two can write your information on the back of a napkin. If he does not want to exchange information, tell him it was nice talking to him and thank him for the dance and great conversation—and then move on. Go back to mingling, dancing, and interacting with other single people who might be more compatible and interested in the things you are interested in.

If you exchange phone numbers or e-mail addresses, however, please follow through within twenty-four hours. Nothing is ruder than to tell someone you are going to contact him or her, and then you take days to make the contact—or you don't make the contact at all. That is disrespectful!

USE A WINGMAN

Using a "wingman" (this term is used to denote either male or female) to help you in social settings is one of the most effective ways to improve your chances of meeting the right person. But it is critically important that your wingman understands his or her role in the process and how to best help you.

You need someone who can help you spot potentially interested parties; someone who may be showing interest in you whom you haven't noticed yet. It is also nice to have someone who can help you assess any interested people. It gives you the confidence of knowing there is someone who knows you and has your best interests at heart. You can also seek your wingman's advice. It is always great to have a second opinion.

Also, a wingman can help boost your confidence and give you feedback as the evening progresses. He or she knows you well and can help push you out of your comfort zone and help you be more open to potential candidates. A wingman also can help you make the connection by introducing you to the person you find interesting by simply saying, "My friend thinks you are very attractive, but she's shy. Can I introduce you two?" It works! But be careful not to pick someone more appealing or charismatic than you are as your wingman because you may be creating your own competition. You can always ask your married friend or one who is in an exclusive relationship to be your wingman to eliminate any competition.

If you decide to leave with your new acquaintance, always tell your wingman where you are going, specifically. Please keep your cell phone handy with your wingman's number on speed dial, just in case things do not go well or get out of hand with your new acquaintance. This is just a good safety precaution.

SUMMARY

You must change your routine to widen your access to potential new partners.

- Adding a cute, adorable dog to your daily walk can be a great attention-getter.
- Walking a child around the park or local populated areas can be a great attention-getter as well.

- Consider taking a dance class, especially Latin, ballroom, or line dancing. You'll meet lots of people who share your interest in dancing.

- Attend a wedding. Women are very hopeful about their future while attending a wedding, and men are reminded that they are becoming the last of their single friends. Both parties tend to be more open and serious about meeting someone special during this time.

- Use a wingman (male or female) to help you find people interested in you at a venue or to provide much-needed advice on what to do next when someone approaches you.

CHAPTER 3

Breaking Down Barriers

I want to discuss a familiar scenario and give you a different perspective and approach to the situation. The scenario focuses on the perceptions and thinking between a man and a woman going to a bar or nightclub.

BREAKING THE ICE

I want to share some striking information I discovered while observing men's initial interactions with women. **Most good men are shy, lack confidence when it comes to women, and *absolutely fear rejection*.** Let's take a look at a typical bar/nightclub scene. This is what many men are thinking about when they find a woman they are attracted to:

- I hope I find some action tonight. (After he spots you …) Wow, check her out!
- I think she's fine, sexy, and really attractive. I'll bet she's fun.
- I wonder if she's interested in meeting me.
- If I make eye contact and smile, will she give me a signal that it is okay to approach her?

- If she smiles back, should I go over there?
- I wonder if she will reject me or embarrass me if say something to her?
- What should I say when I get over there? I am really nervous.
- I think she gave me the eye when I looked over there, but then she suddenly looked away. I am not sure if she's interested.
- She's with her girlfriends; how do I deal with them? How do I separate her from them?
- I just made my approach; I wonder if she likes me.
- Please do not let her embarrass and reject me in front of all of these people.

For most men, especially the good guys, fear of rejection is paramount. Remember, most men have very fragile egos, so please keep this in mind. Some guys are super-confident and suave when they approach you. Be careful of this type—he may be a player.

Faced with the same scenario, many women feel vulnerable, nervous, and unsure of the evening, yet hopeful. Here is what she may be thinking as the night begins to unfold at the nightclub or bar:

- I hope I find someone special tonight; there sure are some cute guys here.
- I just want to have a good time tonight; I hope I meet a nice guy and maybe have a great conversation, a little dancing, and a couple of drinks.
- I am feeling cute and sexy; I hope someone notices my new outfit.
- Oh, I think he's looking right at me; what should I do? I do not want to appear too forward, or easy, or too interested. Should I look away and play coy?

- Oh, I think he's coming over here. How do I look?
- I hope he doesn't say anything stupid or give me some slick or stupid pick-up line.
- Oh, he's cute and well dressed; I love his voice.
- I like his approach. I am intrigued; what should I do?

All over the world, in nightclubs and bars, men and women both are hoping to establish a mutual connection as they struggle to control their nerves and maintain their composure. I call this breaking the ice. Breaking the ice occurs when two people meet and decide they want to get to know each other. Let's start this discussion with the ladies first.

LADIES: You must signal that it is okay to approach you. Remember, most good guys are shy and fear rejection. *So a cute smile, followed by a quick but somewhat lingering glance at him will signal that it is okay to approach you.* He still doesn't know whether you will reject him once he approaches, but at least you will give him the initial confidence he needs to come over and meet you. *Without the signals, most eligible good men will not approach you.* I had a conversation with a couple of gorgeous young ladies recently who rejected this idea. I asked them how many eligible good, nice guys had approached them lately and they responded, "Not many. We always get the jerks or the married ones." My point exactly!

There are some exceptions to this rule, but who wants to miss the chance to meet Mr. Right by waiting for the exception to approach you. So if you like what you see, please give him a clear signal that it is okay to approach you, but do not forget your poise. A simple smile and glance to make eye contact will work. He won't think you are being forward; he will think you are friendly and may be open to his coming over to say hello.

Aggressive, cocky men and players will always approach, but they probably are not the type of man you are looking for—at least, I hope not! They require no signals from you at all. These types of guys love the challenge and the chase. They hope to register new notches on their belts, and you certainly are not that kind of woman, so please stay away from Mr. "Too Cool" or "Too Cute," even if it gives you a thrill. It is not worth the risk and heartache. Bad boys are just that— bad! I discuss how to recognize this type of guy in chapter 9. It will help you determine if you have the right one.

As for the good guys, you put them at ease with a simple smile and a friendly yet deliberate glance. Sometimes you will have to give him several smiles and glances before he gets enough confidence to approach you. The rest should take care of itself. I know you put on your best lipstick, eye makeup, outfit, and shoes before you came out tonight. You have everything going for you. So be confident that the right guy will approach and "wow" you. It's important that you help guys keep hope alive. All good men need is a little encouragement.

Also, there is absolutely nothing wrong with a woman approaching a man who intrigues her and asking his name. There is also nothing wrong with asking a guy if he would like to dance with you. It takes the pressure off him and makes him feel good that you liked him enough to approach. It's okay to try something different to get different results than you are used to.

MEN: Please think about your approach before you make it and be natural. I have surveyed hundreds of women from around the world, and their number-one comment was to please tell men that *women do not like pick-up lines*. I cannot make it any clearer than that, gentlemen. It is important to be friendly, respectful, and sincere when you approach a woman. **Simply say, "Hi, how are you this evening?"** in your best, most confident voice, accompanied by direct eye contact and a soft smile. Then tell her your name and that you are glad to meet her. Ask her for her name, and then repeat her name back to her, shake her hand gently, and repeat how pleased you are to meet her. If she smiles, you have another signal that she may be interested in you. Take your time. Ask her if she is enjoying herself. Ask her what she thinks about the music, the band, or the club or venue.

You are in the discovery phase and need to center your conversation on discovering what you two may have in common. First, take your time to notice what she is drinking (or ask her what she's drinking) and then offer to buy her a drink. A "drink" doesn't necessarily mean alcohol. And please ask her in such a way that she does not feel obligated to you for the rest of the evening.

Women do not like that. You could simply say, "Would it be okay if I bought you a drink? No strings attached!" She will either say yes or no; what do you have to lose?

In my experience, no matter where I've been around the world, women like men who have and use good manners. Being a gentleman is considered quite sexy to many women. It transcends looks in many cases. Remember, women look for men with substance, and the first rule of substance is having good manners. It shows you are more refined than the average guy. It shows you respect her as a person and want to treat her with dignity.

Finding something about her that you can sincerely compliment can be a huge turn-on for most women. Do the unexpected—compliment her on the things she did not think you noticed, like her outfit, her shoes, her glasses, her lipstick, etc. Women love it when you notice that they have taken the extra effort to find a really attractive outfit or beautiful shoes. However, some women are so beautiful you can't help commenting on it. I've been guilty of this one on occasion. Be sure to be tasteful with whatever compliment you give her. I love the words, "You are simply stunning," followed with a compliment about something she's wearing.

LADIES: Please remember the man is trying his hardest to make a favorable impression on you, so accept his compliments and show him that you appreciate his efforts. This will give him the thumbs-up to take it one step farther, such as asking for your phone number or e-mail address or perhaps a date or sharing a cup of coffee.

Remember, you cannot get to know each other unless someone first approaches the other and makes a connection. Here's how to facilitate this:

LADIES: Try your best to be as open and approachable as possible when you are out in a social setting, but always stay classy and refined. You never know who might be the one. If you never let your guard down to send the signals that you are approachable, life will pass by without your ever meeting Mr. Right. I know he is out there waiting to meet you.

How to break the ice: As the interested party approaches, you and your friends should be able to assess his intentions. Watch out for the jerk or player with the smooth pick-up lines. This type tends to get really loud at times, trying to impress the people around him. *If he is a player, a ladies' man, or a jerk, immediately dismiss him—but nicely!* You can simply say, "I am out with my girlfriends tonight, and we are here to have a good time by ourselves. Thank you very much. Enjoy your evening." He will get your point! But if he is a nice, sincere person and appears a little nervous yet intriguing, please set him up for success. All you need to do is be open and friendly. He may or may not be the one, but he might introduce you to one of his friends who may be the one.

If you like the way he approaches you, and he intrigues you:

- Open up to him. ("Hi, how are you tonight? I'm glad to meet you.")
- Extend your hand and tell him your name.
- Be friendly. ("Are you here with friends? Have you been here before?")
- Give him a chance to impress you. Give him a compliment and see how he reacts.
- Tell him if you like the environment (the people, music, band, or venue). ("I love the band this evening. What do you think of them?")
- Ask him to dance, if you like him and his responses so far. I always believe you can learn a lot about a man by watching him dance.

Consider accepting a drink or a cup of coffee, if he offers. If you feel comfortable, you might want to sit down together at a table or have him join you and your friends at your table, but do not let your girlfriends dominate his attention. Remember, he is your guest now.

If you are still comfortable at the end of the evening, consider giving him your e-mail address or cell phone number. I never recommend giving someone your home phone number or address until you really get to know him. I even recommend to my *AskDearlove* clients that they set up a dedicated e-mail address for dating purposes. This e-mail address is separate from their business and personal e-mail accounts. If they decide to stop communicating at a later date, it is much easier to do and it will not impact other e-mail accounts.

MEN: Please be genuine—don't be the jerk that every-
        one hates. She is going to find out who you really
        are sooner or later. Why not be yourself from the
        start? She might really like the real you. Think
        before you approach her. Make sure she is sig-
        naling that it is okay to approach her. Remember
        your manners. Showing her that you have great
        etiquette and poise can be a huge competitive ad-
        vantage. Keep the conversation focused on her.
        The rest will take care of itself. It is important to
        keep things simple.

KEEP IT SIMPLE

Your new outlook on life and increased activity and exposure has finally led you to a promising prospect. Now you
need to remember to always keep your interactions with
people simple, no matter where or how you meet them.

MEN: Please do not bore or overwhelm her with details
        about your job, your cool cars, your homes or
        your accomplishments. Just give her enough de-
        tails for her to become comfortable. Let her ask
        the questions about you. If her questions focus
        on what possessions you have, be careful and
        consider walking away. She is not the one. If her
        questions focus on discovering who you are and
        what you like to do, then answer her questions.
        She is trying to find out if you two have some-
        thing in common.

        Building a connection and potential relationship
        with someone is a journey, and it takes time and
        hard work. Take your time. It is important to build
        trust and to ensure you have a mutual connection

and compatible interests. It is also important for you to be real with each other and maintain honesty, openness, a caring attitude, and genuine concern for one another.

Please do not forget that many women are programmed to expect the worst from men—and we all know why. Surprise her by being consistently different from what her programming tells her to expect from men. This will help her trust and open up to you.

I highly recommend to all my clients that they hold off on sexual relations as long as possible. It may sound archaic, but time has proven that waiting is a very good idea for most couples. Why should you consider waiting to have sex? Because it takes a long time to build a proper foundation, based on shared feelings and love. Sex, for many people, tends to cloud their senses and can monopolize their relationship. Then one day they wake up to discover the only thing they really have in common is great sex. If you are reading this book I hope that you are looking for more in life and from your relationship.

I have found that a relationship built primarily on great sex does not last. Sex, however, is a great enhancer! I recommend you take your time, discover each other, and find out how many different goals and activities you have in common. Many people fail to build and sustain a long-term relationship because they don't like to do the same things. They need shared interests and goals to keep their relationship fresh and exciting. When you like to do the same things and have compatible goals, sex can be a great complement to your relationship. But great sex alone will not sustain a relationship.

LADIES: Please, please, please do not drop all of your problems in your guy's lap. Men simply are not looking to take on all of your problems—they are not programmed that way. So if you approach him with a depressed attitude, anxiety, financial woes, or family problems, you will simply scare him away before anything substantial can develop. Let me introduce you to my friend Marisa and her desires. You'll see how her approach can create barriers and cause her relationships to fail.

My friend Marisa tells me she needs a man who can pay her bills, take care of her, and buy her a nice house and car. She is approaching fifty years old and has never been married. I continually tell her that most men are not looking for a woman to take care of; they are looking for a woman who can fulfill, enhance, and complement their lives, as well as love them. When I ask her what will she bring to the relationship, she tells me that she is bringing her great personality and attractiveness. I think most men are looking for a little more substance today—particularly in more mature relationships.

I believe lasting relationships are built on mutual benefits. This will require some of you to change your game and start showing potential partners the special things you bring to the table. They are so many beautiful, attractive, smart, and engaging women out there today that you simply have to bring more to the table to get the best men. One of the most important things anyone can bring to a relationship is their fun factor. Most people enjoy being around people who are fun and full of life. Showing someone how much fun you are to be with can be a huge competitive advantage.

In addition to the points I mentioned in chapter 1, when it's time to get serious, most upwardly mobile men are looking for a woman who can:

- Complement and enhance their lives
- Support their career success
- Build a successful family and home together
- Build a rewarding and loving life together

I am confident that these are many of the same attributes most women are looking for when choosing their life partner. Guys, remember she is also looking for someone who can complement and enable her life, support her career or job, and build a family and home with, as well as help her enjoy a rewarding, loving life.

Some women have achieved significant career and financial success, but many of them are finding it difficult to attract and find the right partner. This can be quite frustrating for many successful women. I offer the following advice for such women: In my experience of dealing with executive and professional/career-minded women clients and friends, I've learned that many of them unknowingly talk about their jobs, their careers, their workday, and their status. Some like to emphasize that they have their own money and do not need a man to take care of them. That is fabulous and should give women at this level of achievement the confidence, security, and sense of independence they so rightly deserve. But ladies, please do not let this be a barrier between you and the possible man of your dreams. It is critically important for you to *consider choosing someone you feel is your equal*. You want to choose someone who brings the things to your relationship that are important to you and who will complement your lifestyle and career. This type of person will appreciate your success and bring the level of support and love you deserve.

But remember to keep your requirements realistic. Make sure you choose a man who can help anchor your personal life, help keep you grounded, and support your career aspirations. Please don't rule out men who do not make the same amount of money as you do. Some men have other qualities that can enrich your life and make your life easier and more enjoyable. They also may not have the same pressing requirements for their time and therefore may be able to dedicate more time to raising the family and tending to you and your family's daily needs. But I always recommend you find a man with a steady job, no matter what level of achievement he has attained.

Unfortunately, men tend not to want to talk about the woman's job, career, workday, and money. It does not mean they are not interested in what you do and have experienced; they just want to concentrate on something else when they are with you—such as taking you out to dinner, or better yet, making dinner for you or massaging your tired feet and back or making love.

LADIES: Please understand this is a *difference* between men and women. When you ask him how his day was, you really want to know. When most men ask, "How was your day?" they really do not want to know all the details. You need to find someone who appreciates you and all you do and who wants to hear about your day and frustrations. But you cannot vent every day about your day. *No one wants to come home every day to negative conversations and a bad mood. This is true for both men and women.* The key to your relationship's success is finding someone who will be there for you whenever you need him—but understand the limitations of many men.

MEN: Ladies want to talk about what happened during their day, so listen to what they have to say. They will appreciate it, especially when you give positive feedback. But realize that sometimes they just need you to simply listen.

THINK OUT OF THE BOX

Trying to find and attract the right partner is one of the hardest things to do. The reward of finding the right person, however, is more than worth the work—but it will take your thinking out of the box. Consider doing things and going to places you may have only imagined in the past. I found the love of my life five thousand miles away from the United States in Glyfada, Greece. Who would have ever thought? So when I talk about breaking down barriers and thinking out of the box, I really mean thinking out of the box and freeing yourself to experience new people, places and possibilities.

WHERE DO I FIND THE RIGHT PERSON?

The first key to thinking out of the box is to find all the places you can go to meet new people. Let me give you a few examples to get your creative thoughts going. Please consider:

- Taking an adult education or continuing education class on something that interests you. You are sure to find other single people who share similar interests.

- Attending openings, art exhibits, book signings, street festivals, live concerts, and theater performances.

- Taking up a sport or activity like golf, tennis, volleyball, racket ball, bowling, skiing. Many of these activities require partnering and lessons. This can give you the opportunity to meet new and exciting people and potential prospects. The good news is you do not have to bring a partner to the event; they will provide one for you.

- Joining a cycling club, photography group, church group, book club, hiking club, or ski club. Again, each of these clubs will give you the opportunity to meet new people who have some of the same interests.

- Taking dancing lessons, like latin, ballroom, country, or line dancing. You do not need to bring a partner. We have found this to be very successful for our *AskDearlove* clients.

- Attending sporting events, like baseball, basketball, and football games; soccer, volleyball and golf matches. Guys, you won't believe how many single women go to professional baseball and football games until you actually attend one. I was shocked! The stands were full of lovely women of all ages. Ladies, the reverse is also true. So call your local ticket office and get your tickets to the next hot game in town.

- Attending more parties and social events with friends who can introduce you to new friends.

- Taking advantage of outdoor cafes, wine-tasting events, wine bars, community events, or pool parties.

- Volunteering and participating in charity events (Heart Foundation, Race for the Cure, Habitat for Humanity). It is very easy to mingle and potentially meet new friends. You have the opportunity to jog or walk alongside someone exciting for three to five miles. Think of the possibilities!
- Using a professional, highly respected, successful dating/matchmaking service that sponsors and hosts fun, exciting, safe social events.

All of these settings will provide you with the opportunity to meet a lot of new friends and potential prospects who share common interests. So pull out your calendar, start searching the local papers and the Internet, and find the fun events that are happening in your area. Do not hesitate—life is simply too short to put such an important activity on the back burner.

SUMMARY

One of the most productive things you can do is to learn to break down barriers and understand how they are affecting you and your chance of meeting the right person.

- Understand that men and women think differently and may have different expectations when they first meet.
- Learn to manage expectations by the way you communicate and carry yourself (your poise).
- Don't come across as too needy, or you may scare off a potential partner.
- Keep your interactions simple yet stimulating.
- Start adding our recommended list of activities to your event calendar, and begin to enjoy meeting new, interesting people.

- Have faith that your God wants you to be happy, no matter what religion you follow.
- Consider working with a matchmaking specialist to help guide you through this exciting life journey.

CHAPTER 4

The First Call: What Do I Say?

One of the most nerve-racking parts of dating is asking for the date and making the first call to set up your date. This chapter will provide you with the tools you need to build your confidence and master this important dating skill.

Here are several *facts* to remember that will put both of you at ease:

- *Your potential date is as nervous as you are.*
- *Both of you want to make a good impression during the call.*
- *Both of you are worried about what one thinks about the other.*

Let's talk about what the first call is really about. It is a key call that allows you to establish your contact after meeting or being referred to each other by someone you trust. It allows you to verify and build on your first impression, because you now have the time to talk about what you initially discovered you have in common. It sets up your first date and gives you an opportunity to see if you would enjoy that date. It also lets you know your date's taste, based on what he or she suggests for a date. This call allows you to talk in a comfortable environment and get to know the other person. If your call is before the first date, it also gives you the opportunity to change your mind if you feel—for whatever reason—that something about the other person is just not quite right for you. Please make sure, however, that you give the person a chance, and remember that he or she is as nervous as you are at this stage of the connection. And finally, it is critically important for setting the tone of the potential relationship and your interaction with each other.

IF YOU ARE THE ONE MAKING THE CALL

Another important point to discuss concerning your first call is etiquette. Using proper etiquette is the best way to make the right impression and leave someone excited about seeing you and going out on a date. It is time to display your very best manners. When asking for the first date, here are a few things to consider:

- Thank the person you've called for sharing his or her phone number with you.
- Mention how excited you were to meet him or her.
- Be complimentary with something you remember about him or her when you first met.
- Mention how much you have thought about the person since you first met and that you are looking forward to seeing him or her again.

All of these statements let the person know you are really interested without your having to come up with "slick" lines to impress him or her. *Most people do not like slick pick-up lines.* Your prospective date will start to relax and open up more as your conversation continues.

You want to make sure you give the person a chance to tell you how he or she felt about your initial meeting. It is important that you confirm there is a mutual attraction and shared interest between you. Ask what the person has been doing since you last met. Be sure to actively listen to all of the responses. Ask what kinds of things he or she likes to do—hobbies or fun activities. Remember, you want to know how many common interests you two have—the more the better. Talk about some of the things you found out or suspected about him or her from your initial meeting—keep it positive.

Tell her you would like to invite her out on a date, and then describe what you have in mind. Make suggestions, but don't be pushy. You want to take the time beforehand to do your homework and pick a place or activity you are sure the person will enjoy. You should be able to glean from your initial contact or meeting what you share in common. Plan your date around this activity. I recommend not going over the top and keeping your date simple. You don't have to fly her to a private island for dinner to impress her. You can choose a local, popular venue and achieve the same results. Please do not oversell your date. Find out what days and times work best for her, and lock in the date and time.

If you feel she seems noncommittal, ask directly if she is interested in seeing you again. If her schedule is really busy, ask if there is something she would like to do together that would work better with her busy schedule. If so, lock down the date and time. If not, be polite and thank her for her time—and then move on. Life is too short.

IF YOU ARE THE ONE RECEIVING THE FIRST CALL

The first thing you want to do is relax and enjoy your call. If you thought enough of the caller to give out your number, you have probably been waiting in anticipation of his or her first call. *When the phone rings, just be polite and let your potential date know that you are glad to hear from him. Mention how much you enjoyed meeting him and how much fun you had talking to him.*

If the caller asks you about the type of activities you like, please be open. Most people never take the time to ask potential dates what they like to do, so when someone asks, be ready. Let me introduce my friend Georgia and her experience with the first call from a guy she liked.

My friend Georgia is now single after a long relationship. She has been out of the dating game for years. She is tall, beautiful, funny, and extremely successful in her career. When Georgia started to re-enter the dating scene, she discovered her dating skills were not at their best. When the first guy asked her what she likes to do, she found herself tongue-tied and unable to come up with anything to say.

She told me that it had been so long, she wasn't ready for that kind of question. I asked, "Aren't you excited that the guy wants to know what you really like to do?" She said yes, but "Men rarely ask, so I did not have my response ready." I said, "Darling, make sure the next time someone asks, you know exactly what you want to say. If he wants to know what you like to do, know in advance what you like to do. You never know—he may take you on the type of date you have been dreaming about for years. Be prepared and practice."

Men are learning that one of the best ways to impress a woman is to find out what she likes to do and then to put together a great date around that activity. The more interests you have in common, the more things you can potentially share. For example, I love photography and doing photo adventures in exciting places and cities. I can talk about it for hours so I have to realize that the people to whom I'm speaking might not have the same passion for photography. If they do not, I could end up boring them to death. Find out what your potential date likes and doesn't like to do—but take your time. It is all about enjoying the journey and the discovery of each other. Rome wasn't built in a day. The more you know about what the other person likes, the better chance you have for a successful date. It also gives you much more insight into who that person is.

When someone asks if you want to go out on a date, please be polite, even if you're not interested. If you don't want to accept the date, thank the person for asking you and politely decline the invitation. Suggest that you would like to be friends but are not interested in dating at this time—that will send the right message.

But if you have been patiently waiting for this person to ask you out, show enthusiasm about going on a date. Simply say—with some energy in your voice—that you would be happy to go out. Be sure to lock in the date, time, location, and expected dress for your date. Do not be afraid to ask if it is a formal place or more casual one so that you will be dressed appropriately.

I recommend that both parties drive themselves for the first date (and until you are comfortable with the other person). It is a bit too early in the relationship to divulge your address to the other person. Also, please do not go on any date unless you know exactly where you are going. After you are more comfortable and have reached a level of trust with the other person, you can be more open to a surprise date. This is a good safety precaution.

In the early stages of dating someone new, however, I think it is important to tell a close friend or family member where you are going and who you are going with. You may also want to let them know what time your date is scheduled and when you expect to be home. A discreet way of letting them know how things are going during your date is to simply send a text message letting them know you are okay and having a good time (text: *ok gt*). If it is not going well, simply text *"help."* I recommend you set up these messages into your phone before you go out on your date. It will make it easy to quickly and discreetly send the message to your friend or family. It is also a good idea to let your friend or family know that you have arrived safely back home. You know you can't wait to tell friends about your date. Give them a call. This recommendation is particularly applicable to women but applies to men as well.

Even though I do not recommend it, if you decide to spend the night with your new date, please let someone know where you are—just in case there is a problem. And definitely let your friends know when you are back home or at work. Remember, having sex can drastically change the chemistry between two people and often can hamper the development of a strong foundation. But as two adults, you make the call. I personally always liked ladies who made me wait. It is the greatest gift a woman has to give a man, along with her love and trust. My advice to the women is to cherish your gift and make him earn it. My advice to the guys is to not pressure the lady for sex. It could damage or even destroy a potentially great relationship and friendship.

Once you have all the details worked out, simply close the call by thanking the person for calling and letting him or her know you are looking forward to your date. Sound happy and excited, but not over the top. Men love women with energy. Women love men with energy. *No one likes the person who makes the other one work too hard to please the person or to get him or her to smile and be happy.*

At this point, your voice is the only thing you have to impress your date on a call. So be aware of your tone, your mood, your energy, your poise, and your etiquette. This is applicable to men and women, no matter who is making the call and who is receiving the call. Be polished and very polite.

THE FIRST CALL AFTER THE DATE

If you are the host of the date, please remember to call your date and thank her for going out with you. Good dating etiquette recommends you call her the same night, if it is not too late, or the next day at the latest. Tell her you had a great time and thoroughly enjoyed her company. Ask her if she had a good time, and wait for her response. You will be able to tell instantly by the tone and energy in her voice or lack of energy in her voice whether or not she truly enjoyed herself.

If you are receiving positive responses and vibes from your date, tell her you hope to have the pleasure of seeing her again for another fun date. Wait for her response. Talk to her about what you liked most about your date, and ask her what she liked most about your date if she has not already told you. You can talk about memorable moments, comments that stuck in your mind, a specific look she gave you, what she was wearing, her conversation, the venue, etc.

If you are calling the same day or evening after your date, be respectful of her time, especially if she is preparing for or already is in bed. In that case, you can simply say, "Thank you for a great evening. I will call you tomorrow and hope to see you again soon."

As you continue your next call, remember to discuss things you have in common, like hobbies and activities. It is easier to set up another date when you both have things in common that you like to do. It also helps you to continue breaking the ice and discover more about the other's interests. Please do not forget to compliment her again on how she looked, her outfit, shoes, hair, etc. She wants to know that you appreciate the extra effort she put in to prepare for your date. A sincere, compliment can really help build your connection. If you want to compliment her beauty, choose something specific, like her eyes, smile, or hair. And I always recommend you avoid commenting on her body parts at this stage of the dating cycle.

I do think it is okay to ask if she works out, especially if she has a really great body. And if her response is yes, simply say that it really shows. That will get your point across and sound very complimentary. It also gives you another opening for setting up your next date. You can leverage your common interest in working out by perhaps suggesting a date of working out together, or jogging, biking, or tennis. This will build on the connection you already have, as well as show her how much you really have in common.

IF YOU WERE THE ONE ASKED OUT ON THE DATE

You should expect your date to call within the first twenty-four hours. Some people will call the same night if it is not too late and the date went particularly well. However, some men will wait two or more days before calling you, even if it was a great date—I suspect this is due to poor upbringing and a lack of good manners and proper consideration for others.

LADIES: If this is the case with your date, please let him know that it is not acceptable etiquette to wait two or more days before getting back to you. Be polite but honest.

If your date went well and you would like to see him again, tell him how much you enjoyed your date and time with him. Talk about memorable moments and what you liked most about your date together and him. This will open up the conversation and allow the communication to flow between you naturally. You should expect to be asked out on another date, so be prepared. Your goal is to be open to the idea of your next date, and once he asks you, be sure to set up your date, time, and location. Nature will take care of the rest—the excitement will start to flow between you.

Do not forget that men like compliments, too. A genuine compliment about his outfit, shoes, cologne, car, choice of venue, manners, etc., will be well received. You are both well on your way to a great connection.

However, if you did not have a great time, it is okay to say, "Thank you very much for the date, but I am not interested in dating again." Be polite and gracious and then quickly get off the phone. If he continues calling you, and you cannot get him to stop, block his number or change your phone number. This is why I always recommend that people use a different phone and phone number for dating purposes. Please do not lead a person on if you are not interested in dating. Nothing good can ever come from this approach.

SUMMARY

Key Points to Remember

The first call can make both of you nervous; relax and be genuine.

- Remember that each of you is trying to impress the other.
- Each of you is nervous and wondering what the other will say and think about you.
- Be you; be natural.
- Remember your poise, your polish, and your etiquette at all times—it is critical and extremely impressive.
- Plan your date around common interests; it increases your chances for a successful date.
- Be sure you know where you are going and that someone close to you knows as well.
- Plan your call and think about your responses beforehand; show your personality.
- Be sure to follow through after the date and thank each other for the date and time together.

- It is okay to tell each other how you felt about the date and what you think of each other—nothing mushy; be genuine.

- Please call within twenty-four hours of your date; it is just good etiquette and it certainly makes a positive impression on your date.

- Be prepared to ask for another date, and be prepared to accept or decline another date—either way, it is okay.

- Talk about common interests and try to learn more about each other.

- Enjoy your date and future dates.

CHAPTER 5

How to Plan and Create the Perfect Date

PLANNING IS THE KEY

I want to share some words of wisdom with you that have withstood the test of time: "He or she who fails to plan, plans to fail." I personally believe *planning is essential* to creating successful dates. The first part of the planning process is to confirm what your potential date likes to do or places he or she prefers to go. This should be done during your initial meeting or during your first call. You should consider keeping the first date simple, without too many moving parts. The more activities you bunch together into a single date, the greater the chance of something going wrong to spoil the perfect date. A simple romantic lunch or dinner always works.

Yes, lunch is a simple way to break the ice without putting pressure on your date. Dinner often comes with unspoken expectations and may cause your date some uneasiness. Lunch, however, is easier, and seeing each other under the light of day gives you a chance to really check each other out. It also gives you the opportunity to have a pleasant conversation without the other person worrying about what you think will happen after dinner is over.

You want to be sure to plan every detail, from picking up or sending flowers in advance of your date, to opening the door, to pulling out the chair for your date. It is the little things that really matter and will make your date feel extra special. Find out what her favorite types of foods and restaurants or venues are. Once you have that information, you can find and confirm the best place, within your budget, with the best ambience, food, and service. This is critically important. Let me introduce you to my friend Aidan's story.

One time my friend Aidan took a young lady that he really liked to his favorite steak-and-baked-potato restaurant, only to find that she actually only ate sushi. He had no idea that she only liked sushi. Aidan had failed to ask her beforehand what type of foods and venues she preferred and therefore made a bad assumption, which led to a less-than-perfect date.

If your goal is to impress your date, the best way to do that is to ask her in advance what she likes and would prefer. If she responds with something like, "I am easy; I like everything," you might want to press a little harder for her true preferences. If she answers, "Surprise me," then I recommend you pick a nice steak-and-seafood restaurant that has a variety of entrees to choose from. Most people who eat only one type of food will normally tell you, but you might want to check in advance to be sure you get it right.

Do not be afraid to ask her if she is allergic to any particular foods or sauces. This can save you both from embarrassment and give you the opportunity to let your waiter know he needs to pay special care to your date and her allergy.

LADIES: Give the guy some inkling about what you like to eat. He wants to see you eat and feel comfortable at the venue he chooses for the date. Please don't be a bland "salad girl"—men like to see you eat a real meal—but please don't go over the top either. I once took out a young lady who ordered what seemed like everything on the menu. I thought she was starved for food from the way she ate. Remember your etiquette. *This applies to both men and women.*

WHAT MAKES A DATE A "GOOD" DATE?

MEN: Most women like to be romanced and treated special. It starts with how you set up the date. It is important to chat with her until she feels comfortable about going on a date with you. Be a gentleman, and tell her you would like to treat her to a nice lunch or dinner. Once she accepts your offer, please confirm the date, time, and location. Please, please, please do not be late. Being late signals to a woman that you do not think she is important enough to respect her and her time. Do not be late, no matter what. It is a first impression that is really hard to overcome. Let me introduce my friend Henry.

My friend Henry once scheduled a date with a nice lady at a great restaurant that happened to be in an area that was unfamiliar to her and quite a distance from where Henry lived. Henry got stuck in traffic, while she arrived early but could not find the restaurant. Henry had failed to provide clear directions on the restaurant's exact location. It took her fifteen minutes of running around to find the restaurant, and Henry arrived twenty minutes after that. To say she was unimpressed would truly be an understatement. Henry spent the entire date trying to make up for being late. He had to work overtime to impress her with his personality and charisma. Even though Henry delivered his best charm and conversation, she simply sat there with a polite smile. She was clearly upset about how the date started off because of his poor directions and tardiness. Henry never saw her again.

The moral of this story is that good planning is essential to executing the perfect date. Be on time. In fact, get there early to make sure the table is right. Provide your date with clear directions to the exact location of the venue.

It is important when setting up your date that you confirm whether she is meeting you or if you are picking her up for your date. Remember, I always recommend to women that they meet men at the selected venue on the first couple of dates. This is just a safety precaution. If your date is a week or so away, consider sending her a short note to remind her of your date, and let her know how much you are looking forward to it. This will make her feel very special. Women love cards, personal notes, and flowers so do not miss the opportunity to impress her before your scheduled date.

On the day of your date, consider buying her flowers—something creative. A single long-stemmed rose can make her feel really special, especially if you have it delivered to her job. Add a nice box with a bow wrapped around it, and you will really make her feel special. Do not miss leaving a little note card inside—just write something simple, like, "Looking forward to seeing you again" or "I am excited about our date" or "I cannot wait to see you." Any of these comments will make her feel special and heighten her anticipation of seeing you.

You definitely want to call ahead to the restaurant or selected venue to ensure you have a nice table. I always recommend you let the manager or maître d' know you are trying to impress a special lady and would like to arrange for the best table and the most attentive waiter. You should also ask if he can recommend any special desserts, entrees, or drinks.

I always believe you should let your date order whatever she wants, providing she eats it. If she likes lobster, then buy her lobster. Just make sure you are taking her to a place you can afford, no matter what she orders. There are many great restaurants that offer "surf-and-turf" for a reasonable price. Ordering dessert with her is a great idea because it is the favorite part of the meal for many ladies, and they do not like to eat alone with you staring at them. An after-dinner coffee or liqueur (such as Bailey's) can be a great way for you to extend the conversation and the evening. Please do not forget to limit your drinking if you are the one driving. It is a responsible and safe thing to do. You don't want to put your date or anyone else's life in danger by driving under the influence of alcohol.

And finally, please dress to impress. If your dating location calls for casual wear, wear something impressive and stylish—urban chic or classy western wear, depending on where you live. Women just love to see a well-dressed, well-groomed man. They think it is sexy, so please do not disappoint her.

I recently moved to an area where the ladies are extremely well dressed, whether it is a casual or formal setting. The men, however, tend to wear a lot of jeans, with their shirts out, and that is okay. But often, I see them accompanying a beautiful lady who is wearing a gorgeous black dress or dressy outfit.

I personally think that guys need to step it up when their ladies are dressed to impress. A nice pair of slacks with a nice shirt would complement her outfit well. Add a nice tailored jacket, and she will be even more impressed. I may be old-school, but ladies appreciate old-school values.

Now let's get back to planning the perfect date. When she arrives for your date, take the time to notice what she is wearing—her outfit and her shoes. Pay attention to the details; she has spent so much time preparing to be her very best for you. Please do not forget to compliment her. Remember to make eye contact whenever you speak to her, and smile whenever it feels right and appropriate. Women love a man's eyes and smile, and they always take notice of both. If you are waiting outside the restaurant or venue for her, open the door for her when she arrives. Greet her with a big smile and, if appropriate, take her hand in yours and kiss the back of it lightly. She will be very impressed. You may also want to give her a quick hug, but be polite—not too tight or too close.

Once inside, let her walk in front of you as your host or hostess shows you to your special table. Move behind her chair and pull it out just enough for her to sit down, and assist her with pulling it up to the table comfortably. In some higher-end restaurants the host or hostess will assist the lady with her seat. Ask her if she would like to have a cocktail, wine, or simply a glass of water before dinner. Let the waiter know what you two would like to drink. Some ladies prefer to order their own drink and meal; others will want you to choose something for them. Be ready to go either way. Now let the evening flow, and try to keep the focus and conversation on her and her interests.

If you don't know what to talk about, ask questions about what she likes to do or her family or her work. Your goal is to find out as much about her as possible and provide her with just enough information about you for her to determine that you are a good person who respects women and has a solid foundation for your life. You want to pique her interest without boring her with too much detail. She will ask for the details she really wants to know about. *If you find yourself monopolizing the conversation, stop it!*

As the date comes to a close, remember to pull out her chair far enough for her to easily stand up. Thank her for a great evening and for taking the time to share it with you. I recommend you walk her to her car, or ask the valet to order her a taxi or bring her car around. Please open the door for her as she exits the restaurant, and then open the door as she gets into her car or taxi. It is okay to hold her hand and assist her into the vehicle. Do not forget your eye contact and smile. It is the final thing you want her to remember about you—your great smile and eyes.

Please do not push her to extend the evening or for sex at this point in your relationship. Most women won't be open to that approach. They believe that anything worth having is worth waiting for. I happen to agree with them. Waiting for that special time helps build the anticipation and makes the moment so magical when it comes. Some of you want to know if it is okay to kiss her on the first date. After talking to literally thousands of women from all around the world, I recommend that at the end of the date, you kiss her on the back of her hand or on the side of her cheek gently. If she wants more she will initiate it or let you know it is okay. Do not forget to set up your next date, and tell her she can choose where to go.

MEN: **Most important:** Call her later that night to thank her for the date and tell her how much you enjoyed her company. As men, we are not very good with our follow-through with women. So surprise her, and call her that night or first thing in the morning. She is as eager as you are to find out how you felt about your date. Women hate to be left wondering. Pick up the phone and let her know you are highly interested in seeing her again.

LADIES: Thank him for your date and for calling. Let him know you had fun. Be natural and ready to consider what he may suggest for your next date. Guys like knowing that what they have planned is intriguing. Let him know you look forward to seeing him again. This is also a good time to ask any questions you forgot to ask him during your previous date. I sincerely hope you have found a keeper!

MULTIPLE OPTIONS FOR DATES

There are literally thousands of activities from which you can select for your following dates. If you are planning the date, be creative and surprise your partner with something fun and imaginative. It does not have to be expensive. I always recommend that you stick to a dating style that you plan to continue as your relationship grows. Remember the old expression, "The thing it takes to get your baby is the same thing it takes to keep her." You cannot use bait-and-switch type dating styles if you plan to keep your partner long term. Many relationships fail because couples stop doing the very things that brought excitement and fun into their relationship. You have to work hard continuously to keep the fires burning.

Below is a list of simple dates that can start your imagination flowing. But I want you to remember that dating is an art, and practicing the art of dating develops successful dating skills and dates.

Activity	Things to Consider
Restaurant	Choose somewhere classy; know what he or she likes
Sporting event	Make sure he or she likes the sport; mutual interests; buy great seats!
Visit with family	Establish your relationship first; may hurt if too soon!
Outdoor outing	Sailing, picnic, hiking, beach, swimming pool; keep it simple!
Concerts	Get the best seats available (Club level or Concierge Seating); make it special—impress him or her!
Theater	Pick something you know he or she will love; get best seats
Romantic walk	Choose somewhere scenic; hold hands and touch—appropriately!
	Check his or her activity levels and make an appropriate choice of whether he or she will prefer a simple stroll or a strenuous hike.
Shopping	Know his or her taste; go where you can afford! Make it an event; model for each other!
Wine tasting	Be sure the event has his or her favorites; buy him or her a nice bottle or two!
Nightclub or Bar	Choose somewhere classy; upscale; request VIP service if available.
Playing sports	Tennis, golf, racquetball; be yourself; do not show off and don't be overly competitive! Keep it fun!

Date with friends	Make sure they are compatible with your date; be attentive! Do not talk about things with your friends that leave your date out of conversation. See how well he or she fits in with your friends!
Art show; exhibition	Make sure it is tasteful art and a classy affair; dress to impress!
Fun outing	Bowling, playing pool, playing card games, cigar event, photo shoot of scenic location!
Casino night	Fun and exciting time, but could be expensive; date must like gambling! Look for local charity events featuring casino nights, less expensive; more fun!
Cook for him or her	Nothing is more impressive than a home-cooked meal with all the trimmings and attention to detail, if you do not cook, ask your favorite restaurant for butler service at your home to support your date.
Cook for him or her	Nothing is more impressive than a home-cooked meal with all the trimmings and attention to detail, if you do not cook, ask your favorite restaurant for butler service at your home to support your date.

THE PERFECT DATE

You can put together an impressive date with just a little fore-thought and planning, even if you are not an accomplished dater. The following are details for several popular dates:

Go on a Picnic

A picnic is one of the most romantic dates you can ever have, but you have to plan it correctly and pay attention to the smallest details. You might not suspect it, but a simple picnic could be a game-changing move that can really bring you two together—emotionally, spiritually, and lovingly. I believe the most critical part of a successful picnic is to choose the right location. It should be picturesque, serene, fragrant, and capable of creating the perfect setting and the right mood for your date. Try to stay away from locations with screaming children, barking and unleashed dogs, or guys tossing footballs or Frisbees. All of these potential interruptions can be mood-killers and turn the best picnic into a bad experience. Check the area for these types of things before your date. If you are not sure about the area's normal activities and traffic, ask your park ranger.

I like to choose areas that have sun (for sunbathing) and shade (when you need a little relief). It is also a smart idea to check the weather forecast and make sure there is no potential for rain or oppressive heat. It is good to have a backup plan for your date, just in case the weather fails.

Let's talk about the essentials you need to execute the perfect picnic date. These include:

- A soft, clean blanket. Please do not use the one that has been in the back of your car for months.

- Two airline-size pillows to rest your heads on as you gaze at the sky and at each other.

- Ant spray and mosquito repellant—always a good idea to have on any outdoor venture.

- An elegant picnic basket with real plates, bowls, wine glasses, tablecloth, silverware, and napkins. (Many online outlets sell such picnic baskets; it is something you can use over and over again.)

- CDs with music to help set the mood and a small boom box. (Better still: bring CDs of your date's favorite artists and songs.)

- A simple but impressive meal could consist of any of the following items: assortment of sandwiches, finger foods, fruit, assortment of cheeses and crackers, chips, grapes, salad, dessert, wine, bottles of water, ice, soft drinks. Deli sandwiches also work well. Keep it simple, and don't pack too much.

Lay out your blanket and pillows, set up the music, and begin your journey with your special date. When the time is right, open your impressive picnic basket, and pour the wine or other drink. If you are serving white wine or champagne, chill it beforehand or bring a small cooler of ice to keep it chilled. These two beverages are wonderful when served chilled but lose a lot of their appeal when warm.

Prepare your date's plate and ask her what she would prefer on her plate. This is your time to show that you care. It is important to focus on creating the right mood and enjoy the experience so that you can really get into each other.

If you are the guest, let your host know how much you appreciate his choice of location and thank him for the lovely meal. Ask him if he prepared it himself—that will surely get the conversation going. The important thing is that your date thought enough of you to plan and execute what he hopes will be the perfect date—not many people do that these days.

Your date likely will appreciate it if you feed her finger foods or grapes, or if you suggest that she taste different things off your plate. It helps break the ice and allows you two to enjoy a leisurely time together. You can just share and enjoy the moment. If the chemistry is flowing well, it is okay to touch or hold hands as you take in the scenery. Lie back, stare at the sky, and share what you're feeling at the moment. It does not have to be deep thoughts, just honest.

No one likes a messy dining or lounging area (except the ants and flies), so clear up as you finish. Pull out your trash bag, or round up your trash and throw it into a park trashcan.

As your date starts to wind down, continue to talk about the things you have in common and offer suggestions for what might be a great idea for your next date. Help each other load your picnic accessories into the car—and remember to hold hands as you walk back to the car.

I assure you—with 100 percent certainty—that if you follow this prescription for the perfect picnic date, you two will never forget this time together. You will have created a magic moment that you both will always remember.

Cook Dinner

Guys, women love a man who can cook. Ladies, men love a woman who can cook. These are two of the truest statements in the world. Your date will be impressed that you cooked for him or her, especially when you take the time to get all the details right. Imagine the following perfect date, focused on cooking and serving your special person a great meal.

I believe in getting the up-front work correct. I strongly suggest you send your date a formal invitation to dinner—include your address and/or directions. If you really want to impress, send a small bouquet of flowers—or better yet, a single rose—with your dinner invitation. Follow up with a phone call to confirm the date and time, and provide him or her with your home address, if he or she does not already have it. If you don't want to send a formal invitation, you also can call to invite him or her, and follow up with a note and/or flowers.

Before you plan your date, please remember that you should only invite someone to your home after you are very comfortable with that person and have established a basis of trust.

You'll want to dress to impress. You don't have to wear anything formal; urban chic and tastefully casual are fine. But if you really want to impress your date, make it semi-formal or formal. You should use the same approach when getting ready to cook for someone special in your home as you would when taking your date out to an elegant restaurant or venue. Consider preparing something special that you know she will like—you've already done your homework to learn her favorite foods.

You can rarely go wrong by cooking a nice roast dinner with all the trimmings—fish, lamb, or steak; simple vegetable dishes; and a fun dessert. Keep it simple; the more complex you make it, the greater the chance things could go wrong. When you are preparing a special meal for someone, timing is everything, especially if you are preparing a multi-course meal, so plan your schedule precisely. If you do not cook but want to invite your date over for dinner, you can always have a chef come in to prepare a gourmet meal and serve both of you. There are many local chefs and restaurants that offer in-home dining services. Ask your friends for recommendations, check out your local Yellow Pages, or simply Google it.

To ensure a stylish evening that will impress your date, remember to set the table with the following:

- Nice tablecloth (elegant and conservative)
- Centerpiece (bouquet of flowers)
- Matching plates and bowls; complementary silverware
- Water and wine glasses
- Cloth napkins

Your beautiful table settings and linens will truly impress your date. You do not have to have expensive dinnerware and glasses, but you should make sure they match. You may want to add a little candlelight to your table and surrounding room area. I think candles are great for setting the mood in a room. I like to add nice candleholders to my table and then subtly use lightly perfumed candles in the surrounding areas of the room. As an example, the romantic movie *The Holiday* included a romantic home-cooked meal.

Everything is now set and ready for your date to arrive. It is time to focus on creating the mood you want for the evening. Just before your date arrives, turn on a radio station that plays soft music (R&B), soft rock, or pop country, or use your favorite playlist or CD. Your music choice should be in line with your guest's preference for music. Keep the volume low so it can set your mood without it being too loud for you to hear one another. You may want to offer your date a glass of her favorite beverage or a glass of her favorite wine or champagne. If your date has never been to your home, you may want to give her a quick tour of your home. But do not get sidetracked—you know exactly what I mean. And remember to smile.

Pull out the chair to your dinner table and seat your date. If you are the date, please wait to be seated. If you are the host, once your date is seated, unfold her napkin and lay it down in her lap. If the chemistry feels right, drop a soft kiss on her cheek, or better yet, lift her hand and kiss the back of it. You will blow her mind. I admit the kiss on the back of the hand works better for the guy kissing the lady's hand. But ladies, a soft kiss on the cheek as he sits down or a nice squeeze around his broad shoulders will send the message that you think he is important and you're glad he's here.

Walk to your own chair without losing eye contact (perhaps you look away and then look back with a smile), and compliment her on the way she looks under the candlelight. Take the seat that gives you the best view of your lovely date and allows you to communicate easily. Slowly unfold your napkin and pour a glass of wine or your favorite drink. I recommend you raise your glass and toast to a great evening together. Smile and let the journey begin. You may want to take this time to explain what you have prepared for dinner and then begin serving your guest. Your guest may also serve his or her own plate.

Sometimes, if you have a large table that is hard to reach across, it makes more sense to have your guest fill his or her plate. Your eyes and smile can communicate everything you want to say at this point. When you show a nice smile, it lets your date know you are enjoying the evening. If the chemistry is now flowing between you, it's okay to reach out and touch hands during dinner and feed each other small portions off your plates. I recommend you offer your guest something from your plate to taste and see if she reciprocates.

I think it is critical that you make each other laugh, smile, and be comfortable throughout the evening. Consider sharing your day, as long as it is does not create a conversation about work problems. Consider sharing a funny story or how excited you were about cooking for the two of you and sharing this special time together. I believe if you steer your conversations toward discovering and discussing what each other's interests are, you will be best served. People like to talk about things that interest them. They particularly like to talk about their interests with people who share the same interests.

Thank your date for joining you (or if you are the date, thank your host for putting together the fabulous meal). I believe dessert should top off any evening. I have never met a woman who did not enjoy dessert, and I rarely meet a man who will turn down a piece of cake or pie. Dessert puts the finishing touch on the meal. And if you prepare something fun, you can even feed each other dessert. Watch the whipped cream; it can lead to a very fun and imaginative evening. Be prepared. I hope you two create a magical evening together.

If you are trying to think of something special to do for your next date, just cook dinner. I cannot wait to hear about how the evening went. Good luck!

Giselle was working really hard on a project that took her past her normal working hours. By the time Giselle arrived home, she could only stand in front of the refrigerator, staring at the contents, hoping something good would magically appear. In the end she would have a bowl of cereal for dinner. Giselle's boyfriend knew she was going through a really tough week and was exhausted.

He came to pick her up after work one evening. Giselle immediately noticed he had dressed up. He explained he wanted to take her out to a proper dinner, as opposed to cereal and milk, but he had forgotten something at his place, and they had to stop there first. Giselle did not think much of it until they arrived at his apartment, and a man dressed in a tuxedo stood waiting outside her boyfriend's door. The man welcomed them and opened the apartment door. As Giselle stepped inside, she discovered a candlelit table set up just for two. A huge smile came over Giselle's face. Then their host came around and sat them down, poured their drinks, and

> served their food. On top of it all, he served Giselle's
> favorite dish from her favorite restaurant.
>
> Her boyfriend had obviously done his homework. What
> made the date so memorable was not so much that he
> surprised her with a candlelit dinner but the small de-
> tails. He surprised her by contacting a friend and ask-
> ing where would Giselle love to go for dinner. Instead
> of making reservations, he went the extra mile to ex-
> press how special Giselle was to him. He had the res-
> taurant's chef prepare Giselle's favorite meal right at
> home. Giselle still smiles every time she thinks about
> that magical night.

Let me introduce my friend Giselle. You will love her story.

If you do not have the skills to put together an entire meal, be creative—let Giselle's story be your guide. I assure you, your date will think he or she has been crowned king or queen of your heart.

GO TO A LIVE CONCERT OR THEATER PERFORMANCE

If you discover that your special person likes concerts or theater performances, this is an opportunity for you to impress. It does not matter whether you are the woman inviting the guy or the guy inviting the woman, you must get the small details right.

First, I recommend you check out concert and theater schedules in your area well in advance to see if you can find an event that is sure to impress your date. You'll want to start checking early so you are able to secure the tickets and also the best seats you can afford. I think a "combination" date is best, combining dinner with the event. Remember, though, that it is hard to book dinner reservations at popular restaurants near a theater or concert venue when there's a great show in town, so book early.

See my recommendations on how to plan the perfect dinner at a restaurant, and you cannot go wrong. Also try to book club level or box seats or concierge service level tickets at your venue. It is really nice when the wait-service people come to your seats and ask what beverage or snack you and guest would prefer. Check out the venue's service offerings beforehand to see if this level of service is provided. Everyone likes to be pampered, and your date will relish the pampering service and attention. It also keeps you from having to stand in line, waiting to order a drink or snack for your date—that is wasted time you cannot afford to lose. The night is all about your date and showing her a fantastic time. Stay focused—it will pay off in spades.

If you cannot secure this type of seating, floor level seating also can be fantastic, especially if you can secure seats in the first ten to fifteen rows, near the middle or end of the center aisle. You two will be right in the mix of the stage activity and will feel like the performers are performing just for you. The center seats in the balcony or the mezzanine level are fantastic for theater performances.

By now you know to dress to impress, but I want to mention it one more time—it is that important. But you want to be sure to dress appropriately for the occasion.

You might consider a limousine or executive car service for your date, particularly if you both plan to drink or you know that event parking is a nightmare. I went to the Grammy Awards one time and found parking was nonexistent.

Luckily, I'd listened to my brother and booked limousine service for the event. It took us right to the front door red carpet—it does not get any better than that. It allowed us to enjoy the evening well into the night without the worry of finding our car and getting home safely. It may seem slightly expensive, but paying $100–$300 for a limousine or car service is well worth the investment and often makes good sense. Getting stopped by the police after having a few drinks or trying to find your car after the event is over can really stress you and your date. Consider spending the money and enjoying your evening and your special guest.

While riding in the limousine and during the show you will have an excellent opportunity to show the excited and expressive side of your personality. Be yourself, but remember: *moderation is the key to success.* Too much of anything is normally not appreciated. Be smooth, fun, and sexy, but remember your manners. This is especially true for men.

My experience has shown me that a man cannot go wrong by opening doors for his date and letting her go in first. I suggest holding her hand as you walk together. Remember, she spent hours getting ready for this evening; reward her by making her the focus of your night. Guys watching you will like your style, and the ladies will be envious when they see how attentive you are to your date.

I do not see anything wrong with touching each other (appropriately), interacting with each other, dancing together, and holding each other during a concert. I recently saw the R&B artist Maxwell in concert with my wife. She was so excited about it that the energy just flowed through her, from his beginning note to the last note of his final song. We hugged, kissed, danced, touched, and just had a wonderful evening together. Great concerts can bring two people closer, whether they have been together one month or thirty years.

I want to focus on a couple of points. First, enjoy the show and each other. Second, gentlemen please do not let your eyes wander to someone else. It is rude and will immediately turn off your date. Ladies, this is true for you as well. Both of you should remain focused on and admiring each other. If you thought enough to take your date to a live show, please think enough of him or her to make it a night to remember.

I've found that buying a lady a concert program and perhaps a T-shirt with the star's brand on it is very much appreciated and not very expensive. Walk your date out of the venue as if he or she was your king or queen. Make your date feel special, as if he or she is the only person in the world. And finally, do not forget to find something about your date to compliment.

SUMMARY

The Dos and Don'ts of Dating

The key to planning and executing the perfect date really comes down to understanding a few dos and don'ts of dating. People have been dating for centuries, but some things never change. I want to clearly spell out what I know works and what I know does not work when it comes to dating. Remember:

- Dress to impress, and ensure it is appropriate for the occasion.
- Do your homework ahead of time; know what your date likes and then plan accordingly.
- Make your date feel special; he or she will always remember and appreciate it—and you.
- Know your budget, and do not overextend yourself trying to impress. If you plan to use a credit

card, check your availability of funds before your date.

- Most people enjoy simple dates, when they are done well.

- It is imperative to be on time. It says so much about your character.

- Follow up after your dates with a call, note, flowers, text, or e-mail within twenty-four hours after the date. It shows you care.

- If your date went well, ask for the next date. Confirm the date, time, and location. Be creative.

- Never get pushy with your date; it sets a very bad tone for your relationship.

- Notice and read the chemistry between you. Is it really there, or are you imagining it? Make sure it's mutual.

- Please remember your manners; they make a bold statement about who you are.

- Be flexible about changing plans. Things happen that are unavoidable; be prepared to adjust as needed.

- Say what you mean, and mean what you say. Don't make someone try to read between the lines.

- Do not assume the person you are dating has a hidden agenda.

- Whatever you choose to do for your date, make it special—and memorable.

Enjoy yourself, and enjoy your date!

CHAPTER 6

What to Say and Do on a Date

THE RULES OF THE GAME

Everyone wonders what to say on a date to make a good impression on their companion. For some, it comes naturally, but for most people it takes practice—as with anything you want to be really good at. You have been told this your entire life by teachers, parents, coaches, and friends. The rules of the dating game are not any different. *If you want to be good at dating, you have to practice the skills of dating. One such skill is to be natural, comfortable, and real during your date.*

The best thing to talk about is something you both have in common. This eliminates the awkwardness that couples sometimes experience in their early conversations. Your first goal is to uncover what you two have in common. Here are a few proven ideas of how to find out what you need to know.

Let's suppose you find that you and your date have the same hobby or that you like the same music or group. You may even discover that you both like dancing, theater, photography, artists, or sports. It makes it so much easier to talk about something you like and are passionate about. The date and conversation will flow smoothly and comfortably and so will the excitement and chemistry between you.

Let me introduce you to my friend Sandra and her story.

> *My friend Sandra loves line dancing. She recently became an empty nester when her son went off to college. She started going out to the local line-dancing clubs and now has a new group of friends who share her interests. Every night one of her new friends calls and begs her to go out to dance.*
>
> *She told me that she still misses her son a lot, but she has so much to look forward to as she rediscovers her life and passions. Her dating calendar is full with compatible prospects. I'll bet she finds the right person for her after all!*

I am extremely passionate about collecting art and photography. Whenever I meet anyone who likes art or photography, I have a fabulous time talking about our shared passion. The same will work for you! I recently met a young lady who collects art and enjoys photography. We spend hours on the phone talking about techniques, places to shoot, new cameras, lens, etc. This is a thrilling conversation for us, but for someone who does not enjoy photography, this could be a nightmare. So the key is to find something that you and your date both are interested in.

Once you find your common interests, just be yourself. If you are nervous, do not be afraid to share that feeling with your date. He or she is probably as nervous as you are about the date—being nervous is natural. It stems from our internal need to make a good impression. Let your personality flow naturally and everything else will take care of itself. After you have determined your common interests, you can start asking simple questions, like:

- When did you first start [insert hobby, such as traveling, photography, cooking, dancing, playing video games, shooting pool]?
- What do you like most about it?
- Do you spend a lot of your time enjoying [insert hobby]?
- How do you find the time? I am so busy; I struggle to find the time to really enjoy [insert hobby].

These types of questions will definitely spark your conversation. Also tell your date that you would enjoy the chance to share your hobby with him or her. You could also mention how you feel when you are enjoying your hobby—show your passion. People love excited, fun people who are passionate about life and the activities they enjoy. Now that you have determined your common interests, ask simple questions about things related to your common interests.

If your date likes photography, ask if he or she also enjoys paintings or sculptures. You could also ask if he or she collects a particular artist or type of art. You could ask if he or she has a favorite gallery or city for its access to great art. I personally prefer Carmel, California, for it's amazing galleries and access to all types of art and great artists. A little-known fact is that Las Vegas has excellent art galleries with many different types of art and sculptures. I recently found a great local artist in Miami Beach named Andre Allen. His glass-framed contemporary art is amazing and will definitely inspire conversation.

If your date likes to dance, simply ask his or her favorite type of dancing, or how long he or she has been dancing. You should also ask where he or she prefers to go to dance. And guys, nothing is sexier to a woman than a man who knows how to dance. If you cannot dance, sign up with a credible dance studio in your area and learn.

If your date likes the outdoors, ask some of his or her favorite places and activities. *Let your conversation take you naturally to a place where you both feel comfortable.* You will find that your nervousness has subsided and has been replaced with excitement about your shared interests. This really works—practice it the next time you meet someone.

JUST BE NATURAL

I cannot emphasize enough how important it is to be natural. The key is to keep your conversation light, interesting, and funny. Women love men who can make them smile and laugh out loud. Guys, you do not have to be Adam Sandler or George Lopez or Steve Harvey to use your natural sense of humor. You can tell her a funny story about yourself, and she will get a kick out of it. We have all done something embarrassing that other people will find funny. Do not be afraid to reveal that part of yourself. Keep your stories short and engaging, and try to highlight the funny parts. Practice, practice, practice!

Watch your date's body language (and be aware of your own)—you both will send out nonverbal signals. If you see her rolling her eyes, or notice him checking his watch, or if he or she suddenly has a place to go, quickly change what you have been talking about—it is not working! It is time for you to go to Plan B. I suggest you turn the conversation back to your date and let him or her talk for a while. It will give you a chance to recover and also discover a little bit more about your date's interests and likes and dislikes.

Another way to impress is to display etiquette throughout the date. Do not talk while you are chewing food; it is rude. Wait until you swallow your food before you speak. You should engage your date's eyes, lean *slightly* forward, and show her how interested you are in what she has to say. Please be attentive to your date; it will certainly pay off in developing your relationship.

By now if things are going well, you might want to ask a few more personal questions. Say something like, "Where are you from originally? What school did you attend? Did you like it? What was your major?" or "Do you have any brothers or sisters? Are you close to them? Where do they live?" This kind of information will give you a better sense of who your date really is.

Keep your questions light-hearted; you don't want to sound like you are interrogating your date. The more you get to know about a person, the easier it is to discover how many different things you find appealing—or are potential turn-offs. It's also a good idea to ask what types of things he or she likes to do for fun that no one would ever imagine that he or she would do. You will be surprised at some the answers! You can also offer something more personal about you.

Be prepared to share the same type of information about yourself; do not be afraid to share and open up. For instance, after he or she says something that appeals to you, you could say, "I would never have guessed you were interested in that. So am I!" Just be honest about it; don't claim to enjoy something if you really don't.

Try to anticipate your date's needs—this is part of being attentive. For example, if she asks where the ladies room is, find out from the waiter and direct her to it. If you really want to impress your date, stand up and pull out her chair, and when she comes back, pull it out again and help her bring it up to the table. This lets her know you really care about her and whether she is having a good time and enjoying the venue.

I cannot overemphasize how much a sincere compliment can help cement a relationship. There are so many different things about men and women that are attractive. Take the time to discover the things you really like about your date and then take the time to tell him or her. Find your opening and say something such as:

- "I love your suit. It looks great on you! Your tie and handkerchief really accent it well."
- "I love the cologne (or perfume) you are wearing. What is it?"
- "I love that dress on you. You look amazing in it. It is such a great color on you."
- "I love your shoes. They really complement your outfit. I love your sense of style."

Any of these compliments will bring a big smile to your date's face. He or she will be impressed that you noticed and took the time to mention it. This is how you make a lasting impression. A simple, "I love your look tonight" will say it all. You won't need to say anything more after making a statement like that. I call it game, set, and match. Try it!

THINGS TO AVOID DURING YOUR DATE

One of the things I struggle with in any relationship is dominating the conversation. The problem with this is that the person who monopolizes the conversation doesn't learn anything about the other person. If you are like me, you will definitely have to work on breaking this bad habit. It is rude, overbearing, and self-serving. These three characteristics can kill any relationship before it ever gets started. Luckily for me, my wife—then girlfriend—really liked some of my other characteristics and learned to tell me to shut up and listen. Take it from me; it is better to tell yourself to shut up and listen than to hope that your future soul mate has the courage to tell you to shut up before he or she walks out on you.

Your goal is to keep your date talking about herself, her interests, and her family and friends. Ask questions about her dreams, her travel aspirations, her career, and where she sees herself a year and five years from now. Topics to avoid, however, are politics, sex, and religion. These discussions can torpedo your date. People can have such polarizing views about these three topics that I even recommend to my married clients to steer clear of these three topics as much as possible. As time goes on and your comfort level grows, then you will be able to have some great discussions about these three topics.

Once you two decide to become more intimate, you will want to have very open discussions about sex and preferences. But for now, stay focused on building the proper foundation for a lasting relationship. My other taboo topic is profanity. There is a time and place for profanity, but never use it during a date—never! Instead, focus on impressing your date with your mastery of the language and your etiquette. This is what truly impresses people.

Let me reiterate a previous comment: avoid being late. If you are unavoidably detained, please call and explain as soon as possible that you will be late, apologize for the inconvenience, and reassure your date that you are excited about getting together; then tell him or her what time you might arrive. *This falls under the law of "once"*—that is, you can only use this one time. If you are repeatedly late, anyone who cares about mutual respect and trust will ask you not to call again. It will seem that you are not serious enough to respect his or her time and feelings. Being on time helps to establish one of the basic elements of trust— always do what you say you will do!

Another thing to avoid is talking about past relationships. Even when the other person asks you, avoid this topic like the plague. Nothing good can come from this direction in your conversation. First, no one wants to pay the dues for the last person's mistakes. It is not fair to the new person or to you. If it's hard for you to let go (and you feel you have to talk about the past relationship), talk it through with a trusted friend or therapist. Find a counselor who can help you work through the pain and free you to rediscover yourself and your life. Dr. Deborah Johnson, life coach and relationship counselor, has an outstanding book coming out in early 2012 titled *From Breakup to Breakthrough*. Her book offers help for people who are suffering from the hurt and pain from previous relationships. It shows how to recover and return to healthy dating and relationships. In the meantime you have to tuck away the pain and use it as an internal filter for evaluating your new dating partner to make sure you are not repeating the same mistakes, but be open. You might be surprised to find your prayers finally have been answered.

A 2003 study conducted by Louisiana State University reported "88 percent of American men and women between the ages of 20 and 29 believe that they have a soul mate who is waiting for them." You have to adjust your lens, open up your aperture a little, and start to see new possibilities in the new people you meet. By following our proven techniques, you will be sure to find the right one.

Avoid bragging about your accomplishments. Most people like humbleness. It is okay to talk about yourself; just keep it light and short. No one really cares if you were magna cum laude at your school or that you are a vice president at your company or head of the local chamber of commerce. People like ordinary people who have achieved extraordinary things in their lives, but remain humble about them. It is your personality, your charisma, your active listening skills, your trustworthiness, your etiquette, your attentiveness, and your likeability that will score the real points with your date.

I highly suggest you not overindulge with alcoholic drinks. My experience with people and professional matchmaking has shown me that most people are not at their best when drinking alcohol. You want to remain in control and at the top of your game throughout your date. If you want to drink, drink moderately and know your limits. *Please let the concept of moderation be your guide to a great time and date.*

PAYING THE CHECK

There is one final topic I would like to discuss. Often, my clients ask me the absurd question of who pays for the date. I have one simple answer: whoever initiates the date normally pays for the date. I am rather old-fashioned; I believe a man should always pay for a date with his lady, except when she specifically says it's her treat. Let me introduce you to my friend Alexandra's story.

> *My friend Alexandra used a very reputable dating service to find a seemingly great guy. They met for their first date, had great conversation during dinner, and seemed to have good chemistry. When the bill arrived at the end of dinner, the guy asked Alexandra for her credit card. Alexandra was simply stunned and asked why he wanted her credit card. He said that he figured that he would pay half, and she would pay the other half of the bill. Let's just say that this beautiful, successful career woman turned to him with fire in her eyes and abruptly ended the evening. Alexandra, though in her early 30s, is a traditional woman, and most traditional women believe a man should pay when he asks or meets a woman for dinner. Alexandra never contacted him again, nor did she accept any more of his calls.*

MEN: Most women are traditional when it comes to dating. If she is not, she will tell you right up front when you meet her. Some women like to pay or go Dutch (each person pays for his or her own meal). Some women believe that by paying for half of the date, it removes any obligation or expectation of intimacy at the end of the date—respect her belief and intent. But you should assume that if she does not say anything to you up front about paying for her part of the date, you should expect and be prepared to pay.

LADIES: Many of you are accustomed to picking up the check at the end of business meetings with men.

Your dating and personal lives are different from your business life. I think strong, respectful men expect to pay when they take a lady out on a date. Let me reiterate: I believe the lady should pay only when she tells the man that it is her treat. Let me introduce you to my friend Marisol's story.

> *My friend Marisol is CEO and president of her own publishing firm. She is Latino American and extremely well educated, refined, very cute, and likes to have a great time. She tells me that when she goes out on dates or just out with men that she normally picks up the check. She says she is appalled that these men do not pick up the check.*
>
> *I asked her to recount her dates from start to finish. She explained that she likes to meet her date at the venue, which is smart. She and her dates usually have a great time during the meal and over drinks, but when the check comes the guy just sits there with the check still on the table. This makes her feel uncomfortable so she picks up the check and offers to pay, hoping that he will take it from her hands and pay the check. She told me the number of men that let her pay the check often disappoints her. I asked her why she felt compelled to pick up the check and pay it. She explained that she is used to picking up business meal checks, even though when she goes on a date, she thinks the guy should pick up the check.*

I told her that she had a couple of choices. She could establish up front that she is a traditional woman, with all the expectations that go with dating traditional women. Second, she could pay her half of the bill and let him know that he is responsible for his half. But personally, I believe she should let that bill sit on the table and if he does not pick it up, simply tell him she is going to the ladies room and ask him to take care of the bill while she's gone. If he refuses, she is dating the wrong type of man and needs to move on.

A man like the type Marisol dated wants a woman who will take care of him, unless you want to be someone's mother or sugar mama, I suggest you stay away from this type of man. If a man does not respect you enough to buy your dinner, he is simply not the right man for you—period.

SUMMARY

KEYS TO WHAT TO SAY AND DO DURING YOUR DATES

Anyone can master the skills needed to enjoy great dating. All it takes is practice. I have given you some great guidelines as well as specific details to help you with successful dating. The following points are a quick reminder of what you should and shouldn't do during your dates.

- Good dating and communication skills come with practice.
- Be yourself and let the other person see how wonderful you are.
- Date people with whom you have chemistry and mutual interests.
- Talk about what you know; do not try to overly impress your date.
- Keep your conversation light, exciting, and amusing—people like to be entertained and laugh.

- Stay away from talking about potentially volatile topics like politics, religion, and sex.

- Please do not dominate the conversation; focus on asking questions to discover the other person and his or her interests. When responding, keep your answers informative, yet concise.

- Compliment your date; be sincere. Find something you like about him or her to compliment.

- Do not forget to thank your date for spending time with you, and let him or her know you had a great time.

- If your date went well and the chemistry feels good, either of you should feel free to suggest and set up another date.

- The more interests you share, the easier it is to enjoy each other's company and build a lasting relationship.

CHAPTER 7

Poise and Etiquette

WHAT IS POISE?

Throughout this book you have heard me refer to keeping your poise and showing your knowledge of etiquette. Simply put, poise is the way you hold and carry yourself. It is a certain elegance that you have and display. It is the way you hold your head and neck. It is the way you walk, talk, move, and gesture. It is your posture, your hygiene, your clothes, and your style. Poise is dressing the part to fit the occasion. It is being a lady and ladylike, and it is being a gentlemen and acting like one. It is a certain charm that people display; when you interact with them, they come across as confident, pleasant, and assured but not cocky or conceited.

A poised person is in balance and comes across as smooth but not slick. It is being polished, in control, and self-aware, as well as being aware of surroundings and how to fit into them. Poise is portraying the best you can be. I consider a person to have poise when he or she looks and acts classy and displays the proper attitude and behavior toward others.

WHY IS POISE SO IMPORTANT?

Your poise, or lack of it, is the first impression you convey to someone. Most people will formulate their initial judgment about you within five to ten seconds after seeing or meeting you. This impression may be completely right or completely wrong, but history tells us that it is very hard to change someone's mind about you after that initial impression. It is critically important that you remain aware of how you are perceived by others and care about the type of impression you give to others. Let me introduce you to my friend Kerrie.

My friend Kerrie is a beautiful, successful, and extremely well dressed businesswoman. She is known for her poise and etiquette. When I ask my business associates what they think of Kerrie, they respond that she is so confident and strong yet warm; smart yet approachable; well dressed and extremely poised. We love doing business with her. She is so fun to be around.

As a result of her business competency, obvious intelligence, and demonstrated poise, Kerrie has experienced amazing success in the business world. She also has one of the greatest marriages I have ever witnessed. I often turn to Kerrie to mentor young, up-and-coming female and male executives, hoping she can pass on the amazing poise and etiquette that has become her trademark for success.

It takes more than competence, intelligence, and experience to be successful in business and in your private life. Your mastery of poise and etiquette can be the real keys to your success. Display your poise in every situation; it should be a priority in your life.

I want to address our younger men and women: Many of them have adopted the style of wearing no belt or shoelaces, or the style of allowing their thongs to show or wearing their pants halfway down their butts with underwear showing.

LADIES: If you believe a man who dresses in the above fashion will be able to provide a good life for you and provide you with a safe, nice home in a great neighborhood, please think again. His lack of poise and self-respect are manifested in the way he carries himself. He looks like a thug, whether or not he actually is one. Many people's first impression of him is one of fear and flight. Even though this may be a popular style among some of America's youth and young adults, it creates a negative impression on many people. The guy may actually be a great person, but a lot of society will not give him the chance to prove it.

Caring about how you impress others is very important to your ability to create and establish successful, rewarding relationships. When a woman first checks out a man, she immediately runs him through her filters. She wants to be impressed in such a way that she feels he could be a good candidate for a great relationship, potential marriage, and raising a family together. Unfortunately, if a man is not poised, he may never receive the chance to meet the woman.

MEN: If you are into women who like to wear very low-cut pants that display their thongs, even when they are not bending over, let me assure you that she will bring you more problems than success in your private and work lives. You need a woman who dresses appropriately and carries and represents herself well in all settings, not one who displays that you have questionable taste and make poor choices. Any woman can be sexy *without* displaying her thong.

WHAT CAN POISE DO FOR YOU?

When you have poise, it establishes and controls your internal and external filters. It makes you think about how something you do or say will be perceived before you do it. It helps you cast yourself in the best light so people can see what a good person you are and enjoy being around you. Poise helps you to not come off as brash, arrogant, or lacking class. There's nothing worse than creating an image that makes people not want to be around you because they fear you will embarrass them and yourself. Let me introduce my friend Steve and his story.

My friend Steve's dad, God bless him, has a love affair with alcohol. Ordinarily, he is one of the most charming, witty, and gregarious men you would ever want to meet. But when he adds alcohol to the mix, he loses his poise and charm and makes people not want to be around him for fear of him embarrassing himself and them. This has hurt all of his relationships over the years. Take a lesson from my friend's dad: do not ever lose your poise and charming ways, not even for a moment. The cost is too high.

Poise is not something you are born with, and it is never too late to be taught poise and to master how to use it in your everyday life. It can be a game-changing skill, especially in relationship building. Seek out someone you admire for her poise, and ask her to mentor you, or simply emulate her behavior and learn to carry yourself well. People who have great poise are easy to spot. They radiate like no other in the room. This is true for both men and women.

WHAT IS ETIQUETTE?

Etiquette is showing and having respect for the people around you and the environment you are in; it is all about having and using your manners. It's remembering to say please and thank you. It is opening the door and allowing someone to walk in before you, especially if it is a woman. It is addressing and talking to your date or partner with respect and being courteous. It is being genuine, compelling, funny, engaging, and maintaining your focus and attention on your date or partner. It is not using curse words or inflammatory remarks that can offend other people. It is when you defer your opinion or action in favor of someone else's option or action. Etiquette is also refraining from displaying flamboyant behavior that makes others uncomfortable. It is just being polite and cognizant of other people's feelings.

In all my years of coaching people, the one thing I have found that impresses both men and women is a person who understands etiquette. It is so refreshing to see someone display good manners and good judgment. It is more fun when you go somewhere and do not find anyone saying inappropriate things or dressing inappropriately for the occasion.

Admittedly, it is getting harder to find places where etiquette is the norm, but there are still places where people treat each other with respect and dress to impress. Society has developed standards of behavior for various social settings and situations. At one time, parents, neighbors, schools, and coaches all worked together to help children learn and practice these expected standards of behavior. But we are not seeing this same emphasis as much as we used to. Therefore, it is crucial that you know what these behavioral standards are and then master them.

Good etiquette is showing that you have good manners—just simple, good manners and not stuffy or snobbish behavior. No one likes a snob except another snob.

Here are some simple basics to remember:

- Know how to set a formal table and which silverware to use for certain purposes.
- Place a napkin in your lap before dining. I always like to ask for two so I can wipe my mouth with one while the other one remains in my lap.
- Do not grunt or groan while eating your food. There's nothing wrong, however, with telling your date that the food is absolutely superb.
- Pass the food around the table to make sure everyone has a portion before starting to eat. Begin eating after everyone has been served.
- Pull out a lady's chair and assist her with pulling it up to the table. This one will earn you more points with a woman than you can imagine. Ladies, do not be afraid to ask your gentlemen to assist you with your seat. His response and actions will tell you a great deal about his personality and how he feels toward you. Remember, you are looking for someone who makes you feel special, not just another guy like the last guy with no manners.
- Know how to order at a restaurant. Please tip when it's called for and thank the waiter when you receive excellent service. Standard tipping practices are different all around the world. In America,

standard tipping is 20 percent of the price of the meal. Europe, Asia, and South America are quite a bit different, so please check before you dine in these countries.

- Honor women by opening doors and letting them enter first. Walk a woman to her car to ensure her safety. Open and hold her car door open until she is safely seated and then close it.

- Always thank someone who has gone out of the way to please you, either on a date or by providing you with great service. It is just good etiquette.

- Help elderly people or people in need of assistance to cross the street, or help them with their groceries or packages. It might be your mom or dad or grandma or granddad who needs assistance one day, and you will hope someone returns the courtesy to them.

- Help people in need put their suitcase or carry-on luggage into the overhead of a plane, train, or bus.

- Give up your seat to the elderly or a person in need, a child, a pregnant lady, or a woman. It is just the right thing to do.

- Wear your clothes appropriately, and try to impress those around you with your excellent taste in fashion. Display your manners.

As these behaviors become part of your daily routine, your date or partner will notice that you are really a good person and one worth keeping. Why not spend the extra effort? It will only take you seconds to do something good for someone else and sincerely impress your date or partner.

WHY IS ETIQUETTE SO IMPORTANT?

I believe displaying great etiquette can separate you from the masses of people who do not practice good etiquette. Our society has learned to accept a certain amount of rudeness and inappropriateness, but I do not believe there is any room for it in personal relationships and marriage. I believe etiquette makes you more attractive to others and especially to potential partners. It opens doors for you and provides access to more opportunities, both in your work and personal life. You become a beacon for how someone should behave and for what is appropriate. God knows, there are too few good role models out there today, especially for our young adults and teenagers.

Good etiquette helps you come across more professional, polished, well trained, and well spoken. I can still remember the time my older sister Debbie went out on a date and told us when she returned home, "He opened the door for me and pulled out my chair. He blew my mind! No man has ever done that for me." That simple gesture by her date made her feel special, like a princess. My brother and I learned that day how important it was to open the door for ladies and help them with their chairs at the table. That lesson has paid off for the two of us more times than we can count.

People are not born with poise or understanding etiquette; they are taught these skills. The key is to master these skills and then display them as part of your everyday life. They become a part of who you are. If your parents did not teach and reinforce these skills, it is not too late to learn. All it takes is practice, practice, and more practice.

You can use the following poise and etiquette chart as a quick reminder. I highly recommend you master the dos and don'ts. It could make all the difference in your personal and work lives.

Poise and Etiquette — Dos and Don'ts

DOs	DON'Ts
Carry and represent yourself well.	Don't embarrass yourself & others!
Make a good first impression.	Don't come off as a jerk or snotty; first impressions count—huge!
Be classy; be a gentlemen & a lady.	Don't come across trashy, brash, untrained or tacky!
Dress appropriate to fit the occasion. It creates a great impression!	Don't over or under dress! Know what's appropriate for your environment!
Check with hosts to see what is expected.	Don't just show up and risk embarrassment.
Work to fit in and blend into the environment. Learn to socialize and interact well!	Don't be the one no one wants to see show up at the event.
Be respectful to others always!	Don't show your ignorance and lack of exposure.
Use your good manners always!	Don't be disrespectful; it does not win friends or impress people—ever!
Help people that need assistance.	Don't sit there and ignore someone in need of help; it is poor etiquette.
Use your poise & etiquette to gain advantage.	Don't let your lack of poise & etiquette hurt you & your relationships.
Greet people professionally & with class; endearments are okay to use with partner.	Do not use slang to greet people; it makes a bad impression.
Lead by example; especially for younger people.	Don't send the wrong messages with your behavior. Check yourself!
Be charming, confident, assured.	Don't come across cocky, conceited, slick or uppity.
Keep your internal & external filters engaged!	Don't let your mouth or behavior find you trouble!

DOs	DON'Ts
Always make and maintain eye contact with people.	Don't look away, look down or check out someone else; it is rude and lacks respect for your date!
Be attentive on your date & always keep him or her as your primary and sole focus!	Don't act disinterested; stay focused!
Make sure your dating partner is right for you.	Don't stay if your date is not going well, thank them & excuse yourself.
Let your date know you are really into him or her & the date.	Don't take or make phone calls or fidget with your watch or act disinterested.
Be pleasant, warm and nice.	Don't be cold, unpleasant, or rude; it never works out to anyone's benefit.

SUMMARY

The dating market is highly competitive, and you need every advantage possible to find the right person. Your poise will allow you to show why you are such a fantastic catch and potential partner. Your etiquette makes you attractive to be around. Poise and etiquette can make the difference—just ask your friends of the opposite sex.

Poise and etiquette are learned behaviors—and it is never too late to learn and master them. I have heard so many men and women tell me, "I am just who I am, and I cannot change." *If you want to change your life, you have to change your attitude and add new skills.* That is a simple fact. You never know who is watching you or checking you out, so always be on top of your game. How you meet and greet people tells them a lot about you. Send out the right messages and nonverbal communication (body language), even when you do not know someone is checking you out.

CHAPTER 8

Dressing to Impress

FIRST IMPRESSIONS

Let's revisit the important topic of first impressions. People tend to notice your hair, clothes, shoes, makeup, facial hair, and other features before they even speak to you or acknowledge that they are checking you out. Now let me ask you: What does your look say to the world about you? Are you sending the right message?

It is unfair, but people evaluate and form opinions about you based on what they see. To make sure you are always making a good impression, you have to put forward the best you possible—always! It takes serious introspection to determine what you really want to say through your chosen look. You have to be able to step back and look at yourself from someone else's viewpoint and then be honest with yourself. Your chosen look and the way you carry yourself is your first message to the world about who you are. People will remember you based on what they see and hear from you, so it is crucial to get this part right. It is also the easiest part to get right.

DRESSING TO IMPRESS —
WHAT DOES IT REALLY MEAN?

When you think of dressing to impress someone, all sort of images and questions come to mind. Do I have to look like the cover of those dreadful magazines with supermodels plastered across their covers? The answer is no, you do not, but you do have to consider what subtle changes you can make that will really help you stand out in a crowd and get you noticed—and it's more than just the clothes you choose to wear. It is your entire look, but that doesn't mean you have to become a fashion princess or prince. It also does not mean you have to start dressing flashy or flamboyantly. What it does mean is you should *dress in a way that creates a memorable and favorable impression*, especially on the people you are interested in impressing.

How do you determine which look will give people a favorable impression? You may love the way you look, but you are not trying to attract and impress yourself. You are trying to find someone new to share your magic moments and perhaps the rest of your life. Look around and observe what other people are wearing. Do they appear attractive to you? Also, listen to what people say about the appearance and behavior of others around you. If they have favorable comments, ask yourself why they are impressed with this person—or ask them why they are impressed. If their comments are negative, ask yourself why they have such a negative impression of the person. And again, you can always ask them why they feel that way. This will give you a quick lesson in how people form opinions of other people, even people they do not know but just observe.

BUT I DON'T HAVE WHAT IT TAKES

It does not matter what size, shape, or height you are; you can always make yourself more attractive to others. If you think you are not as pretty or as handsome as other people, commit this next comment to memory: being beautiful or handsome will only get a person the first glance over other people in the crowd, but it is not enough!

Once people start to talk to you, they will quickly look for substance, confidence, etiquette, personality, and compatibility. None of these qualities have anything to do with being born beautiful or handsome. These are qualities anyone can master and use to their advantage—anyone! These are the qualities that can be real differentiators for you and become your competitive advantage.

How many times have you seen an ordinary-looking guy or girl with someone super-attractive and wondered, "How in the world did he get her?" or "How did she ever get him?" Maybe the beautiful or handsome person was attracted to the poise, personality, and openness of the one who might not be so physically attractive. Great beauty will attract attention, but it still takes great manners, poise, caring, and a good heart to impress someone long-term. These are all things within your control. I also believe a person's personality and *fun factor* are huge distinguishing factors.

Let's talk about the norm as well as the beautiful. There is little real difference between what we have to do to win at dating and build relationships and lasting marriages, regardless of outward appearance. Being born beautiful or exceptionally handsome does not give you an advantage in finding the right person and building a lasting, rewarding relationship and or marriage. Becoming the best all-around person you can be will definitely help in this area.

You have to learn to *accentuate your positives,* whatever they are. *Everyone has them!* Ask yourself, "What is it about me that someone else would be interested in or find attractive?" Once you figure it out, accept it and learn how to work it. If you are too modest, you may have to ask a friend or loved one to help you discover what is best about you. They can give you their opinion so you can compare their input to your own. They may point out something great about you that you never recognized.

It's a little-known fact, but many people are afraid to approach extremely attractive people. *Never* count yourself out! Instead, you should work on making yourself as attractive as you possibly can and then let your personality, good heart, and lovely spirit do the rest. Don't be afraid to approach and say hello to someone you find extremely beautiful or handsome. You may be the only nice person to approach him or her in ages. Remember that jerks, players, and gold-diggers always go after highly attractive people. Consequently, highly attractive people are tired of this type of person and may be extremely impressed to meet someone as real and genuine as you. Just because someone has great looks does not necessarily make him or her a good partner. It's his or her personality, poise, etiquette, compatibility, honesty, and commitment that is important, not his or her looks.

For some odd reason, I always had guy friends who were tall, dark, and handsome. I am short, dark, and okay-looking. In my younger life, I always wished I had their features. I thought they had better hair, better skin tone, better height, and better physiques than I did. But you know, over the years of hanging out with them, I learned that because they had so many attractive physical features going for them, they never took the time to develop the whole package. Their personalities were okay and their substance, particularly around women, was okay, but they were masters of the one-night stand. Now that we are all much older and their great looks have started to fade, some of them are discovering that it takes substance to attract real women.

I, on the other hand, found the girl of my dreams and married one of the most beautiful women in the world. I found what my competitive advantages were and figured out what positives I could hone and accentuate in my interactions with women and other people. I have enjoyed a rich life, both personally and professionally. I owe it to the principles I am putting forth in this book.

Anyone can win in life. You just have to believe in yourself and accentuate the best things you have to offer. Charisma, enthusiasm, a great smile, good style, poise and etiquette, and substance can take you a long way in life and in your relationships with people.

You do not have to be born beautiful or handsome to win in life. True beauty is in your heart, your mind, and your spirit; it's in the way you carry yourself, your chosen look, your substance, and the way you treat others. And luckily for all of us, these are things we can all control and improve. Let's start on some of the obvious changes you can make.

GET RID OF THE DATED LOOK

One of my favorite shows on television is called *What Not to Wear*. The hosts, Stacy London and Clinton Kelly, are fashion-makeover experts. I find myself captivated as

I watch it. The show's concept is that a friend or family member contacts Stacy and Clinton about someone who desperately needs a makeover. Stacy and Clinton then approach the person to offer a fashion makeover—on the condition that he or she agrees to give up all his or her old, outdated clothing. A team of makeover experts then helps transform the person into the most attractive person he or she can be. Remember, anyone can look good by paying attention to the right details—*clothing, accessories, attitude, and overall appearance.*

Really evaluate yourself to make sure your style and overall look correspond to the times. Are you still wearing some of the same clothes you wore in high school or college or when you were much younger? If so, it is time for a change. Do you still have the same hairstyle from your younger years? It may be time to make a change.

We always tell our clients, "Change yourself, and you will change your life for the better." Consider going to a personal wardrobe shopper who can help you choose the best look to accent your best features. He or she will relish the opportunity to help you dress and unveil the new you. You can also ask a friend who has an eye for fashion to help you update your look.

When picking out a new wardrobe, consider versatility. There are basic pieces of clothing and accessories that, when put together, can allow you to build several different outfits by just mixing and matching. Tim Gunn, fashion TV host and author, has a great book on how to put together complementary outfits using ten basic pieces. I recommend you purchase a copy of his book—*Tim Gunn: A Guide to Quality, Taste and Style*—to help guide you. You definitely want to make sure your fashion and look fit the environment you are in. You wouldn't wear an "after-six" formal outfit to perform daily duties. You also wouldn't want to wear your daily work clothes to the company's Christmas party or a formal event. If your company supports business casual dress, do not go to work in your daily-chores outfit.

Business casual dress can also be highly effective at impressing a new date. It is just a matter of good taste and determining what is appropriate for the occasion and location.

Most women love to see a man wearing a well-fitting suit and complementary shirt with an open collar for a dinner date. **Most men** would love to see a woman in a tailored skirt or slacks and a complementary blouse or a beautiful, well-fitting dress when they go out on their date. Remember, how you look impacts how you feel, and it also sends a huge message.

I worked as a consultant to some of the greatest multinational companies in the world and have seen very inappropriate clothing on some of the employees over the years. This was particularly true when many major companies decided to convert to business-casual dress. Many people still have a hard time trying to figure out what is appropriate for business-casual dress.

I still am surprised when I look around in restaurants, concert venues, exhibitions, nightclubs, or theaters and see what people are wearing. I firmly believe that good style and what to wear for specific occasions should be taught to everyone. It should start with the parents' and loved ones' guidance, but our system has broken down over the years; this is evident by the look some people portray to the world each time they step outdoors.

We all can help improve the look of today's young people. If we take the time to dress appropriately and to impress, we will send a powerful message to our young adults and children. People mimic what they see. Let's set the right examples!

Let's start with the **ladies**. Women should determine if they need to update their hair and makeup. Hair and makeup styles change regularly, sometimes quite dramatically. Who can forget the beehive hairstyle and the deep, dark eyeliner of the '60s or the wild hair of multiple colors, styles, and textures of the '70s and '80s? Even though these were very popular styles, they are not the best look for you today.

Ask your hairstylist for a more modern hairstyle that accentuates your face—this is especially good advice for all the ladies who have very long hair covering half of their faces. Your hair is hiding some of your best features, like your eyes, cheekbones, and smile. If you are going to wear long hair, make sure it is healthy, styled, and well taken care of. Little turns off a man faster than long, frizzy, dry hair. There are so many hair commercials on television showing models with fabulous styles of shiny, healthy hair that it sets an expectation for what hair should look like. Many women choose to add more length and texture to their hair using hair extensions or other sophisticated techniques. All I will say is that most men like to run their hands through your hair. It will be hard for him to do this if your hair has extensions, nor will you want him to. I personally like short, sophisticated cuts on women. It accentuates and shows off their eyes, cheekbones, and lips.

You don't need to have model-like hair, but you certainly can have healthy, well-groomed hair. You might want to consider a new cut, a new style, adding a hint of color, or a complete color change. But I believe you should always rely on hair-care professionals to help you with your new changes. Also you may want to take a style-conscious friend with you for advice and feedback.

While you are at the salon or at your local department store makeup counter, consider having a makeup specialist update your makeup (e.g., color, tones, eye shadow, lip gloss). If you are having it done at a department store, your makeover is usually free, but they expect you to purchase the products they used and recommend for your face. I think that is a very good deal. You also might want to use a makeover specialist who works with you to transform your entire look to include fashion and makeup. They are worth the cost and time; and you will never forget your experience with them. If you don't have the money in your budget to hire one, take one of your stylish friends with you to make suggestions.

Men, too, should update their hairstyle in keeping with the times. If you still go to a local barber, it may be time to consider going to a professional hairstylist to update your look. Many barbers are quite capable of giving you a great style and cut, of course, but if your barber is not one of them, consider making a change.

You also might consider adding a hint of color to your hair, particularly if it would accentuate your face and features. For men with African American-type hair, the ladies always love a trimmed, lined, and well-cut style that features your rows of waves. Do not miss the chance to sport your waves.

It is common to hear ladies ask why men who are balding grow long hair on the sides of their heads and then comb it over the top to hide their baldness. My best friend used to say, "If you cannot fix it, feature it." Keep your hair well groomed, and if your head shape supports a bald look, consider shaving off all your hair. Many women think clean-shaven heads are sexy.

I also recommend getting your beard and mustache professionally shaped and trimmed to give you a clean-cut look. Women usually do not like the scruffy or un-kempt beard look. As you get a little older, don't forget to check your nose hairs, eyebrows, and ears for excess hair that may need trimming. Just the other night, my beauti-ful wife stared at me and said, "Honey, you need to trim those long gray nose hairs. They do not look very nice." I was quite thankful that she told me, but I was also really embarrassed, because I should have checked to ensure my total look was at its best.

Men, always check and recheck. One day you will find that you have an abundance of hair growing out of your nose, eyebrows, and ears that you never had to worry about before. Keep it in check and well groomed. And you certainly want to avoid the unibrow look—that's when your eyebrows grow together and connect in the middle. Get your eyebrows professionally done and cleaned up. Most pedicure and manicure salons also offer eyebrow-waxing services that can eliminate this problem.

DRESS APPROPRIATELY!

No matter who you are or what type of body shape you have, you should always dress appropriately for your size, shape, and age. For years, my friend Martha has been try-ing to convince her daughter that she wears a size 12, but she actually looks great and more comfortable wearing sizes 14 and 16, depending on the cut and fit. Many peo-ple have a strange concept of what size they should be and will force their bodies into clothes that are not the right size, even if it is not flattering.

You either have to lose the weight or convince yourself to move up to the more appropriate size. No one likes to see the "extra bits" bulging out of someone's clothes. This is a really important point when it comes to dressing to impress and applies to both men and women. *Buy clothes that fit your body.* Please do not stuff yourself into clothes that are too small. They will make you appear much larger than you really are. If you have a large or less-than-flattering midsection, consider wearing shirts and blouses that cover your midsection without clinging to it. Choosing clothes that properly fit your size and body type will give you the best look and make you appear much slimmer and well groomed.

Many people would not consider a miniskirt age-appropriate on women over fifty years old. But I think most people would appreciate seeing these women wearing well-fitted dresses and skirts that fall two or three inches above the knees or at the knees. It actually makes you look quite sexy! Also, adding color and popular prints to your wardrobe is a great attention-grabber.

Even if you are a young woman with a great body, you still want to exercise some discretion when choosing the length of your dresses and skirts. There is a fine line between being cute and sexy and being inappropriate. What message do you want to send the person you are trying to attract? Leave something to the imagination; don't share and show all your best assets up front.

It may sound conservative, but when a man is looking for a woman to commit his life to, he's not thinking about the girls who show him their underwear because their outfits are always too short. He is looking for someone he can take home and get approval from Mom, Grandma, Dad, and his sisters. Will your outfits pass the test?

Tight-fitting pants may not be the best look on most women or men, but there is nothing wrong with wearing tailored pants that properly accentuate your body shape. Again, it is a matter of style and appropriateness. If you are not sure what to buy, take one of your girl or guy friends or sisters or brothers with you. Just make sure they have a great sense of style and fashion. You also could rely on a professional personal shopper to assist you.

LADIES: If you do not have the waistline you wish you had, choose stylish clothes that downplay your waistline. Consider dresses with an empire waistline. Don't choose overflowing dresses; one that is cut trimly will accentuate your best features. If you have a large bust, wear clothes that adequately cover but still accentuate your top half. Also, make sure you wear the right size undergarments for your body type. It helps your clothes fit and look better on you.

One of my friends is about five feet tall, but she has a large bustline. She found the best way to increase her comfort level was to go to a store that employs a professional who is trained to measure women's bodies for the correct size and style of undergarments. It not only made her feel better in her clothes, but her clothes fit better, too. On the other hand, if you are a smaller woman, there is nothing wrong with using a push-up bra to enhance your look. The push-up bras today are so elegant and stylish that they will make you feel like you are wearing a million-dollar outfit.

MEN: Ensure that your shirts and pants cover all the parts they are supposed to cover. Nothing impresses more than well-fitting, stylish clothes on a well-groomed man. When you dress age- and size-appropriate you send the world a clear message about who you are—you are a well-groomed, confident person who enjoys dressing well and looking your best. Everyone appreciates your effort, and many will let you know with a quick nod or an actual comment. When someone compliments me on my clothes or look, I still get boyish chills and feel like I can conquer the world.

Dressing age- and size-appropriate gives you the best chance of leaving a favorable, lasting impression on others. Remember, men, it is very hard to qualify for well-paying jobs when you are dressed inappropriately. Don't you believe it is worth the tiny effort required to make dressing to impress a priority and reality in your daily life? I sure do!

COLOR MAKES A STATEMENT!

Nothing says more about you than the colors and patterns you wear. It is your signature style (or lack of style, in some cases). Muted, understated color might blend you into the background, particularly in a crowd of people. If your goal is to attract the right person, you cannot do so if he or she can't find you. You want to be noticeable, even in a crowd—but in the right way.

Wearing stylish clothes in tasteful shades of color helps you stand out and gets you noticed in a good way. If you choose to wear bold, flamboyant, over-the-top clothes, they also will get you noticed, but it may not be in a good way. I see flamboyant, over-the-top dress as symptomatic of personality issues, like a lack of confidence or a cry for attention. When it comes to dressing to impress, you are trying to attract attention from the right person. If you are not getting the results you would like to have, consider wearing a new look and see what happens.

I believe accessories complement a nice outfit like a beautiful frame complements a great painting. I love to see women wearing a nice scarf, attractive shoes, a designer handbag, and a colorful or diamond necklace and earrings. It says so much about her and how she feels about herself. It also makes her stand out in a crowd. I always notice the shoes and the accessories and a well-fitting outfit. In fact, my wife whacks me sometimes because I cannot help complimenting a woman who has taken the extra steps to complete her look. It may get me into trouble, but it sure puts a smile on the woman's face when I compliment her. I think well-dressed women, even in casual clothes, are true works of art, meant for all to enjoy their sense of style and beauty. I really mean it!

Guys, women will tell you that a tasteful colored or patterned shirt, a complementary tie, an accent handkerchief, a nice vest or sweater, and tailored jacket or suit can do a lot to impress them. If you live in an area where western wear or the rugged look is the norm, buy quality outfits that enhance your appeal. And please pay attention to the fit of your jeans. It's important that they fit well and accent your overall look. Many women love the look of the urban cowboy, and there are some great jeans and cowboy boots available.

Accessories make you stand out in a crowd of men wearing suits or casual wear. Women love to see tasteful jewelry on a man, like a fashionable ring, watch, or bracelet, but keep it conservative. Remember, you are not dressing to impress the guys; you are trying to impress the ladies. I like to wear an elegant watch (not expensive), ring, and bracelet, and I always get compliments from people about my accessories. You don't have to spend a fortune for good accessories. Most large department stores and jewelry stores carry great, affordable accessories, particularly in the silver and stainless steel jewelry lines. Take a look! I personally like David Yurman's collection of men's accessories.

SHOES MAKE THE PERSON

One of my most favorite topics to discuss is how to pick out great shoes to accentuate your outfits. I believe shoes make the person. Why? If you pick out the best outfit to wear, but your shoes are not in good repair, polished, or in keeping with modern fashion, people will notice. You could be wearing an expensive outfit, but if your shoes do not complement what you are wearing, most people will notice your shoes and not the outfit. It's very easy to take your outfit to a quality shoe store and get their specialists to help you pick out shoes that will complement your outfit and enhance your overall look.

Women often judge men by the shoes they wear—and vice versa. So with so much riding on your ability to attract the right person, please take the time to shop for a pair of comfortable yet timeless shoes. Some styles never go out of fashion—these should be the mainstay of your wardrobe.

Some shoes might seem pricey, but if you take care of them, you will be protecting your investment for years to come. It is very easy to keep them polished and ensure the heels, soles, and overall shoes are in good repair. There are shoe repair shops everywhere, and most top hotels and airports have shoeshine professionals. Take advantage of their expert services. Do not forget your etiquette; please tip them well. I always add a $10 tip to my bill for shoe-shine services.

Do you know the difference between fashion-conscious shoes and fashion-forward shoes? Fashion-conscious shoes will remain fashionable for many years to come. Fashion-forward shoes come out every year and have a fashion life span of about one to three years. You can add a couple of fashion-forward shoes to your shoe wardrobe every year, but remember that fashion-conscious shoes never go out of fashion. For instance, ladies high-heeled pumps have been in fashion for decades and are still one of the best ways to highlight an outfit, as well as your legs and feet. Fashionable sandals can be excellent additions to your wardrobe, but often change styles every year.

Dressy shoes can do the same for men. Women are impressed when men wear polished dress shoes with their suits or business-casual clothes. Casual shoes complement your more casual outfits, but they often vary from season to season. Make sure you are wearing shoes that are still in fashion. In my younger days, many men wore shoes that had stacked heels and soles. Today, it would look ridiculous to wear that type of shoes. Take the effort to update your shoe wardrobe. Shoe colors can be seasonal and fashion-forward. Be sure the color of the shoes you are wearing matches the season as well as your outfit.

Shoe comfort is important, too. A cheap pair of shoes can hurt your feet and cause you foot issues like blisters, corns, and bunions. I always suggest that you spend a little more for your shoes to ensure you have the right size and fit. Let me introduce you to my friend Craig.

> My friend Craig would always come to work complaining about how much his feet ached. Craig is about six foot four and weighs about 200 pounds. I asked him where he normally purchases his shoes and did not recognize the store as one that I would normally recommend to my clients. I took Craig shopping at Johnston & Murphy shoe store. Their shoe-fitting expert measured his feet from all angles and recommended the best type of shoes for him.
>
> Craig turned to me and said, "But these shoes are expensive," and I said, "So are your feet, especially if you have to have them operated on as a result of wearing cheap shoes." I explained that a good pair of well-fitting, moderately priced shoes normally costs $100 to $300. Craig tried on several pairs of J&M shoes and began to smile and talk about the fit and comfort.
>
> He purchased three pairs of shoes that day and hasn't complained about his feet hurting in years. He buys his shoes only from J&M, and he receives compliments from the ladies all the time. He says it was definitely worth paying the extra money for the comfort, fit, style, and quality.
>
> Now whenever I meet people with shoe-comfort issues, I always tell them to add $100 to $200 to the price they normally pay for shoes, and the problem will go away. However, some very pricey shoes are not very comfortable. Please try them on; walk around the store to check the comfort level and fit before you purchase any pair of shoes.

Moral of the story: take care of your feet by wearing high-quality but moderately priced shoes ($100–$300 for men and $70–$300 for women), and your feet will take care of you.

Tennis shoes are great for sports and casual outfits, but it is critically important that you keep them clean and in good repair. Everyone needs a pair of white tennis shoes—they can really set off your casual wear and sportswear.

DRESS CLOTHES REALLY IMPRESS

I really believe when you take the time to dress up, it impresses people. I talk to a lot of people every day about many of the topics in this book, but dressing up and style are my favorite discussion topics. Many of the people I talk to say they feel better when they are dressed up in a special outfit. Many women cannot resist noticing a well-dressed man. They particularly like to see a man in a classy, well-fitted suit, tie, and dress shoes.

Many men cannot resist noticing a woman in an attractive suit, great-fitting dress, or classy skirt and blouse, accompanied by a pair of attention-grabbing, cute shoes. And who can resist a woman in an elegant evening gown or a man in a black tuxedo and tie?

I have met many people over the years who say they do not like to dress up. They prefer to wear jeans or casual clothes all the time. I only ask them one question: "How is that working for you?" Remember, if you are attracting the type of person you are interested in, then don't change a thing. But if you are not having much luck finding and dating the right partner, you might want to consider changing to see if your luck improves.

You do not have to dress elegantly; you just need to find a new look that works for you and attracts the type of person you are looking for. I believe nothing is more noticeable than changing your look. Let me repeat: if you want to change your life, update your look!

CASUAL CLOTHES CAN ALSO IMPRESS

Everyone needs to relax, dress down, and show a lighter side of their personality. I believe wearing the right casual clothes can accomplish this. Here a few key points to wearing casual clothes to impress:

- Ensure your casual clothes still send out the right impression.
- Ensure your casual clothes are appropriate for the event or place; it is easier to dress down if you're overdressed than to dress up if you are underdressed.
- Ensure your casual clothes are in good taste and are age and size-appropriate.
- Ensure your casual clothes are up-to-date and in fashion, not your old blue jeans and cutoffs from college or high school or ten years ago.

There is a big difference between casual and business casual; the latter is much more formal than simple casual dress. "Business casual" normally means no tie but a nice jacket, slacks, and polo or open-collar shirt for men; and dress pants and skirts with a nice top for women.

Casual clothes can be very impressive if you take your time and coordinate your outfit well. Pay special attention to your selection of blue jeans. They come in every possible price range and styles, so there really isn't any reason why you cannot select a pair of jeans. Be sure, however, to choose the right jeans and fit for your body shape.

Ladies, there is nothing sexy about jeans that do not fit you properly. Men, there is nothing sexy about your jeans hanging too low and showing your underwear or sagging well below your butt. Jeans can complement your wardrobe and style, so take the time to get the right fit and style. Jeans are versatile, especially when you add a complementary jacket to complete your ensemble; it takes your look to a new level. But remember, most men and women like to check out how your jeans fit in the rear. Be sure to look in the mirror to ensure the fit of your jeans accentuates one of your best features. If you are not sure, take someone with you who is fashion wise.

SUMMARY

The New You

I hope you realize that you are just a decision away from attracting the attention you want and living the life you deserve. All you have to do is commit to learning how to make a good impression and then put your new skills to work. Remember the power of using your eyes, your smile, and your personality and that the clothes always make a statement about you—dress to impress as part of your everyday life. Remember, too, that you should make the *right* statement to achieve the results you want. (If you are the only person who is impressed by your style and dress, you will be a very lonely person.)

Also remember that wearing the right colors can make your appearance come alive and stand out. And finally, re-member the importance of adding accessories to comple-ment your look. Good luck as you introduce the world and your friends to the new you.

CHAPTER 9

How Do I Know
If I Have the "Right" One?

One day you wake up happy, smiling, singing, and maybe even dancing and realize something has changed in your life. You find yourself thinking about a certain person all the time. You believe you have finally found your ideal life partner. At this point, you two have had a number of very successful dates. You love spending time together and enjoy each other's company. You begin thinking it may be time to take the relationship to the next level. But you are extremely nervous and wonder if your partner is feeling the same way about you and the relationship. What do you do?

Well, here's some brain-rattling advice: ask him how he feels about you and your relationship. I believe having open and honest communication is the most important foundation to building a strong, lasting relationship. So many relationships go awry because people simply won't talk about the things they are wondering about or that bother them.

Open and honest communication allows you to stay on the same page—in sync! It keeps you in tune to what each other is feeling, thinking, need, and want. It also helps ensure that you have the right person.

What defines the right person? That, my dear friends, is the million-dollar question. In chapter 1, I asked you to do an honest assessment of yourself; to clearly determine what is important to you in a partner and how important certain characteristics and traits are to you. Let's review this assessment in more detail. I personally believe most people's relationships fail because they *do not know what they are looking for*. They find that they quickly fall for someone's good looks and charm or the attention they receive, but soon afterward, they discover that their relationship is failing, or they are becoming bored.

I believe if you take the time up front to do the prep work, you can break this cycle, find better potential partners, and be able to choose the "right one" to build a successful relationship. So what is required to make all of this happen? You must determine what you want and need from another person to make you happy, excited, comfortable, and attracted. In addition to the qualities and traits we discussed in chapter 1, I also recommend you strongly consider:

- Attitude toward children or desire to have children. It is critical that you know and accept this answer before committing to anyone.
- Social level. How important is this to you? Will the person be accepted in your social circles? Will you be accepted in his or hers?
- Compatibility. Does the person like to do the type of things that are important to you (and vice versa)?
- Marital status. Do you care if someone is divorced or widowed, or would you prefer someone who has never married?

- Career and financial status. Is the person employed and financially stable or between jobs? (This is a huge one.)
- Life goals and aspirations. Are the person's goals and aspirations compatible with yours? Will he or she support your goals as well?
- Have you determined what type of behaviors or things you absolutely will not put up with, based on past experience or your personal preferences?

If you were honest in your assessment, you have put together the best profile for helping you select the right compatible partner and to validate your choice. We are all human; we have emotions, and many times *our emotions will get in the way of the facts* so that we do not see as clearly as we should. We meet someone attractive, and all of a sudden our filters falter. We find that we have become so impressed by the physical attributes or a single trait that we do not process the whole person through our compatibility filter. Let me introduce my friend Diane and her story.

My friend Diane met a great up-and-coming young man early in her life. They had a great relationship that was full of fun! One day after they were married, Diane noticed that even though they were unbelievably compatible in their sex lives, her great husband never wanted to do anything when he got home from work except eat dinner and watch TV. She found that his interests during the week also carried over to their weekends together. She frequently asked her husband to go on a fun trip, or out to dinner and a show, or just go out with friends. He would always respond that he was too tired. Diane is ten years younger than her husband and still has a zest for life and doing exciting things. Her husband no longer shared the same interest in going out and traveling as Diane had.

> *Even though they had an amazing sex life, Diane soon discovered that she needed much more than great sex. In fact, she needed a partner who wanted to share in the activities and interests that she had. As you can imagine, they ended their relationship in divorce. Diane still says it was the greatest sex of her life, but she does not regret moving on with her life and finding people and partners who liked to do the same fun and exciting things she likes to do and expects as part of her personal relationships.*

Diane let the powerful lure of great sex highly influence her decision to get married. You might ask, "So what's wrong with great sex?" Nothing! However, time revealed that the two of them really had very little in common other than great sex. It is critically important that you process the whole person through your compatibility filter.

Before you commit and find yourself in a similar position, find some restraint or have someone talk some sense into your thinking. The reason you invested all the time and painstaking trouble to develop an ideal partner profile was to significantly improve your ability to recognize and select the right person for you. So take advantage of it.

Being with someone might feel good now, but you want it to feel good for a lifetime. Don't "settle." My daughter once told me that her greatest worry is that she won't be married by the time she turns thirty years old. I told her that her greatest worry should be that she finds out she has married or committed to the wrong person—no matter what age she is. If you think you have found the right person, you must process the whole person through your ideal compatibility profile and through your personal filters. They are part of your check and balance system.

Once you have done that, you can honestly determine if you have the right person. This is your best way to avoid a letdown or broken heart. Please re-read this paragraph again—it is that important!

Remember that people show you the parts they believe you will be attracted to. *It may or may not be the real person.* Over time, you will see all the parts and traits unfold, and you can assess who that person really is. How long will it take before you can be sure you have seen all of that person? Only you will know, but I believe you will see most of any person within six to twelve months of steady dating.

Sometimes it will take less time for you to become comfortable with a person and know in your heart that you have found the right one. In that case, make sure the relationship feels right and that you both believe you are a good match and have many things in common. Still, the key is that you *actually share those experiences together* and enjoy each other's company. If so, you have the recipe for keeping your relationship fresh, fun, and exciting. Remember, though, that some people like the same things but prefer to share those experiences with their friends and family, rather than their mates—be very aware of this and make sure your opinions on this are the same.

Take your time. Life is not a sprint; it is a journey to enjoy. Sometimes you will get it right, and sometimes you won't. The key is to learn from your experiences and adjusting your filter and radar to detect early on those who are not right for you. You do not want to find yourself constantly saying, "I should have known. All the signs were there." Processing your potential life partner through your compatibility profile filter can save you from making a mistake over and over again. Let me introduce a great story about my friend Gary and his daughter's fiancé, Jesse.

> *My friend Gary's daughter is a beautiful interracial woman. She is charismatic, highly intelligent, loving, hard working, and honest—the ideal woman. One day, her boyfriend, Jesse, came to Gary to ask for her hand in marriage. Gary liked the young man and thought he would be a great match for his daughter, but he knew Jesse would need some help to make it work long term. Gary and his wife had really spoiled their daughter over the years and knew it would take a special man to keep her in check while making her happy. So Gary asked Jesse, "How well do you know my daughter?" He said, "I love her, sir, and she is beautiful, smart, exotic, and witty." Gary smiled and said, "Let me share a few pointers with you, if I may."*
>
> *Gary said, "Son, my daughter is a princess—and you haven't met the princess yet. My daughter is in the close-the-deal stage of your relationship. You are seeing the best that she can possibly be, but once you get married, you will meet the princess and all her expectations, which will be many." Jesse laughed but took note.*
>
> *Jesse and Gary's daughter have been together for seven years and married for five. And Jesse now knows who the princess is and, thank God, he still loves and appreciates her for who she really is.*

People unveil themselves a little at a time. They want to impress you and make you like them. It is so important that you ask the right questions and get the answers to be comfortable with them. You may be betting your entire future and life on them.

You might consider double-dating with your potential partner's friends so you can learn more about her and see her in different environments. I also recommend spending time with the person and his family as well. You can learn a great deal in these environments. Take the time to know him and see how much you really have in common. The more things you share in common, the better chance you have of making a relationship work.

When you have to constantly seek others to share in the activities you like to do, it puts gaps in your relationship, and over time it can make it seem stale and boring. Make sure you have found your soul mate by taking him through your compatibility filter and being strong enough to walk away if he does not quite measure up. Make sure you are being reasonable as well. Let me introduce some wisdom from the master of personal and professional success, Warren Buffett.

Warren Buffett once told an audience at Columbia Business School that the biggest key to a successful life was choosing the right life partner. He said if you get that one wrong, everything else goes wrong. I think these are unbelievably wise words from a successful businessman, husband, and father. I also believe choosing the right partner is the most critical decision you will ever make in your life. It establishes the foundation and direction for your future life, family, and aspirations.

Take your time in evaluating and choosing your partner, but do not doubt yourself and your ability to select the right partner. Sometimes when you take the person through your filter, he won't measure up against all your criteria. That is when you have to know how to apply your *close-enough* filter.

There is no such thing as the perfect person; therefore, there is no perfect match. But you certainly can get it close enough that it feels like the perfect match for you.

Only you can make that decision, but you can also ask your trusted friends and family for help, and then trust your heart and instincts. There is a right one for you—but there is no *perfect* one for you.

It takes a while to build a good foundation, but it is definitely worth the investment of your time. I always recommend that you state your expectations early in your relationship and let your partner know what outcome you expect and your time frame for making it happen. Let me introduce my friend Julie.

My friend Julie is a beautiful, energetic, funny, and smart young lady. She moved in with her boyfriend when she was twenty-one years old, expecting to get married. Every year they talked about getting married, but he never seemed to commit to a date. The last time I saw Julie, she was twenty-nine years old. She had finally moved out of the house with her boyfriend, because he never popped the marriage question, even though he had enjoyed all the benefits of her living with him and taking care of him and his needs.

Julie found the strength to walk away after sacrificing nine of the most precious years of her young adult life. She is now thirty years old, bitter yet still hoping to find the right partner to marry. She tells me that all the thirty-year-old guys want to date and marry twenty-somethings. She does not feel as confident about finding the right person now that she is thirty. Once she recovers and starts to date again, I'm confident she will not repeat this mistake. I am also confident that there are plenty of men looking for women in their thirties who can complete their life.

Establish up front what you expect from your relationship and do not compromise based on false promises—this is crucial. Some people have a hard time committing to marriage, so if marriage is your goal, make sure it is also your partner's goal. You also have to make sure you both share the same timeline for making it happen. Otherwise, you could find yourself frustrated, disappointed, and much older. Don't be afraid to set clear expectations—and walk away if they are not met.

Let me introduce you to my friend Mandy. Her story is definitely a wake-up call for women who want a family with children.

Mandy was a very successful teacher in her thirties. She always liked the energy and free-spirit attitude of younger men. She found the younger man of her dreams in Roger. Roger was a successful restaurateur in Tulsa. He was full of life and had the carefree attitude Mandy liked in men. He was twenty-three years old when they first met. They quickly fell in love and decided to move in together.

After seven years they decided to have a child together, but were unsuccessful. During that same period, Roger decided that he was too young to get married and start having children. Mandy and Roger broke up after eight years, without ever conceiving a child together. Mandy still wants to have a child and now wants to find the right person to marry. She is now forty years old.

The moral of this story is to make sure you have compatible dreams and goals. Mandy spent eight years hoping that her partner's goals and life plans would finally merge with hers.

Put limitations on how long you plan to wait for the major milestones in your relationship to occur. Even though, Roger was successful and had the right personality and attitude for Mandy, that same carefree attitude would not allow Roger to make the type of serious commitment Mandy ultimately wanted. Her clock was ticking for starting a family and his hadn't even started. Once it did enter his mind, he realized he wasn't ready for either marriage or children. It is critically important to be on the same page about the major things involved in a relationship—especially when it comes to marriage and children.

Now let me introduce you to my friend Tori, who got it right!

After facing the ups and downs of dating, Tori reached the point where she was content with being single. Once she was comfortable and embraced the idea of being single and not feeling the pressure of marriage, she learned to approach relationships quite differently. So when Tori met George later in the year, she was super-confident with herself and carried her new outlook into their first date. She considered a relationship as nice to have, but no longer felt that marriage was essential to complete her already successful life.

When she first met George, Tori thought he was just like the others, and she was determined not to make the same mistakes of her past. She set very clear expectations up front with him that she was not interested in games. She also explained she was not going to become involved with someone if it wasn't going to be a serious relationship.

She explained that if she did get involved, she fully expected that after one year, their relationship would result in marriage or end in a break up. Tori had become very frustrated with past long-term relationships that were filled with empty promises and false hopes. She was now thirty years old. George was very interested in Tori and committed to pursuing her with the full understanding of her expectations and her timeline.

They took their first few dates very slow and spent the first few months building a strong friendship and sharing common interests as their foundation. After six months, they became much more serious and in little over a year, George proposed to Tori. George and Tori were married the following year, and they have been happily married for close to three years now.

I have talked to hundreds of people over the years that tell me they spent their best years with the wrong person and that it took them too long to realize that they had incompatible goals or were being strung along. You cannot get time back, so make the most out of it by ensuring you both are on the same page. Tori sure did, and it paid off huge for her. Although she was very content to stay single and enjoy life with her friends and family, she had to admit it was so nice to have someone special to share her life and special moments.

TAKE THE TIME TO KNOW EACH OTHER

It is always a good idea to take the time to really get to know each other. You may want to consider taking vacations together away from your familiar environment and daily influences. You will see how well you get along and how much you enjoy each other's company. Or you may find you are not as compatible as you once thought. If your culture and personal beliefs are not in conflict, you may want to consider living together for three to six months once you reach the serious stage of your relationship. For some people, this is a good idea before committing to a lifetime together. It certainly worked for my wife and me.

Please recognize that living together definitely is not for everyone. But if you do decide to live together, make sure you have an agreed-upon expectation of marriage or exclusivity, and a time frame for it to happen. Some partners will string you along, promising marriage, to get you to move in with them. Once you move in, many partners are less motivated to actually marry you. I recommend you get the ring and set the date before you commit to living together. If you both agree that all you want is a long-term, exclusive relationship, then that is a different story. But make sure you both are on the same page with your expectations. I believe the same compatibility and selection rules apply no matter which way you want to go with your relationship. I believe you particularly should discuss the idea of bringing children into your relationship, especially if one of you already has children.

It is very hard for someone to fool you for six to twelve months about who he or she really is. This is especially true if you are dating regularly and do not have a long-distance relationship. The real person and his or her intentions will emerge, in most cases, during that time frame. Look for inconsistencies in the things he says and what he actually does. You also get to see her personal habits, hygiene, and daily interaction with you. This will help you determine if you can deal with these parts of her, and vice versa. Also remember, people can change over time. Regular communication and the willingness to compromise are the best ways to keep your relationship and your love intact.

There are certain things, however, that you do not want to deal with. Most people do not consider these things until it is too late. It's important to determine what those things are. Decide how you feel about your partner's:

- Housekeeping habits
- Personal hygiene

- Snoring
- Drinking habit
- Drug use
- Infidelity
- Lying
- Bad temper
- Career or job commitments
- Couch-potato habit
- TV remote hogging
- Timeliness
- Any other annoying behaviors

At the beginning of your relationship, you are so excited about being together that you think of little else. But the above-listed points are important to consider—they have contributed to real tension and even breakups between two loving people. Let me introduce you to my friend Marcus and his story.

My friend Marcus recently married after a whirlwind romance with his fiancée, Fiona. They spent the better part of two years flying back and forth to meet and share time together. Marcus worked in Chicago, and Fiona lived in Nashville. They met during a conference and took an immediate liking to each other. Whenever they spent time together they found themselves cracking up at each other's jokes and constantly laughing. They loved being together. They started to take small trips together and developed a more serious relationship.

After some time together, Marcus noticed that Fiona snored—and loudly! But he thought he would get used to it. Then they decided to get married. They are now married and living together in Nashville, and Marcus still complains about Fiona's loud snoring.

He says it keeps him awake, and he often has to go sleep in another room. Marcus is now finding that there are several other little things about Fiona that also annoy him, and he wishes he had discovered these things before making his decision to take their relationship to the next level. He still loves her deeply, so compromise may be the best way for him to go.

Remember, you have to evaluate the whole person. Sometimes it's the little things that bring tension into a relationship. You need to discover as much about a person's habits as you do about his or her heart and aspirations.

Make sure you can continue to love and live with him or her, even when you have to deal with little annoyances. Grown people rarely, if ever, change their habits. My wife and I both snore. We just nudge each other until we stop, and then the next day we lovingly talk about each other's snoring—I tell her she cut up all the wood in the house last night with her snoring, and she tells me to shut up because I snore like a freight train and scare all the dogs in the neighborhood. Now that is what I call compatibility! We simply accept our faults and move on.

You must learn from your past experiences and incorporate those experiences into your selection and decision process. Don't try to force something that does not fit. You have to remember what things or behaviors adversely impacted your previous relationships and take them into account. Life is too short to settle for being in a bad relationship with someone who does not respect you or support your goals and wishes.

Please do not go into a relationship with the expectation that you will change your partner. This is the biggest mistake made in relationships today. Here is an important revelation: *people do not change who they basically are.*

Too many people make the mistake of thinking they can change someone who is really not right for them, but this is not going to happen—not ever! Just take your time and find the right person!

I know it is hard sometimes, but you have to remain confident that you will find the right person. Take your time, use your partner compatibility profile, and be honest with yourself. *God made someone for each and every one of us.* I really believe this, and you need to believe it as well. The challenge for you is to go out there and find that person. You also must realize that the right person is not going to come knocking on your door, in most cases. You have to go out there and be active. Put yourself in the right environments to meet the kind of person you prefer. You will usually discover him or her doing activities you enjoy doing. But if not, change your routine.

You also have to be realistic about what you want in a partner. Are your expectations reasonable? I can tell you from a man's perspective that the first woman who meets his compatibility profile and has the fewest demands is the one who normally wins. It may not be fair, but it represents how many men think. If a guy is looking for a long-term partner, and one potential partner has twenty different demands he has to meet, and another one has ten demands, there is a good chance he will pick the one who has fewer demands.

The key is to know what you want from a relationship and understand that your requirements have to be reasonable to another person. If your past relationships ended because someone couldn't or wouldn't meet your expectations, then you should strongly consider updating your compatibility profile and choosing a different type of person. How many times do people find themselves repeatedly choosing the same old loser-type they picked before? The funny thing is they actually expect to get a different result from the new but similar relationship. *If you keep doing more of the same thing, you will continue to get more of the same results.* If you do not want to continue ending up with partners who lead you to heartbreak, unhappiness, and feelings of failure, *break the cycle.*

Start by changing yourself. Modify your compatibility profile and turn to someone you trust to help you find, filter, and select the right partner. Matchmaking professionals can make the process of clearly identifying the right type of person easier and show you better ways to find that person.

Sit down with your closest advisers or seek a matchmaking professional's help for an honest assessment. They can provide valuable feedback on any potential partner you are considering for a serious relationship. Do not discount what they tell you. They will always have your best interests at heart. They often can see things and pick up on things that you may not notice.

Your partner should fit well into your social circle, and you should fit well into his or hers. Once you feel the relationship is ready, spend some quality time with your close friends and family, and see how well things go—this will tell you a lot about the future of your relationship. Not many relationships can survive when your close family and friends do not like or accept your partner. You can still make it work, but it is extremely hard and requires you to reinvent your life and support system. So if your partner does not seem to fit, find out why—and then be open and honest with yourself and accept feedback from those closest to you.

WHAT ARE YOU REALLY LOOKING FOR?

My clients and friends often ask, "What am I really looking for in a partner? It is so hard to get it right. And how can I be sure that I have found the right one?" The following table provides some suggestions that you may want to consider:

Does your partner	√
Make you and your happiness a main priority in his life and find a way to balance his work commitments and the quality time he spends with you?	
Have financial stability and proven capability of contributing to the financial commitments of your relationship?	
Respect you and your feelings and does not yell at you or cause you harm or belittle you?	
Complement you and enhance your life?	
Bring out the best in you and make you feel good about yourself and your life together?	
Value the special things about you that make you unique, attractive, and desirable? And vice versa?	
Like to do many of the same things you enjoy doing and make sharing time together fun and exciting?	
Have the same or a compatible value system as yours? (You know what's important to each other and share many of the same ideas about life, finances, and responsibilities.)	
Share your family values and attitude toward raising children and building a family together? (If he already has children or you already have children, do you both agree on how you will support the children, emotionally and financially, and their activities? Do you agree to limit the drama from your ex-husband or ex-wife [the children's father or mother] in your relationship?)	
Share and support the same life goals and aspirations? (And are you on the same page about how to get there?)	
Provide the love, friendship, companionship and nurturing expected from your soul mate?	
Fit your criteria for the right partner? (And do you also fit his or hers?)	

The bottom line is that you want someone who truly makes your life better, someone you cannot imagine living your life without. He or she makes you feel good about yourself and your future life together. After you consider your responses honestly, you will have a great idea of whether you have the right person. I hope you noticed that physical attributes are not mentioned as part of the criteria for determining if you have the right partner. I'm not saying they are not important, but I will say they are not as important as the criteria I've listed in the table. If you believe you have found a good person with a good heart who treats you well (emotionally, physically and financially), the other things may not seem as important.

DETERMINE WHAT YOU DON'T WANT

Don't forget to review the list of things you cannot deal with, and evaluate him or her against that as well. This is critical! Remember, it is always the little things that make or break a relationship. If you have found the person who meets your criteria, and you his or hers, you have found magic. Embrace him or her, and let your lives begin. But if you find yourself sad, crying, or constantly making excuses for him or her, you have the wrong person. *Time will not solve that problem; it will only magnify it.* You must believe that you deserve to be happy and that the right person is out there waiting for you. *Do not settle for less!*

Many of you find it difficult to find exactly what you are looking for. This can put you in a vulnerable position sometimes and can cause you to pick the wrong person simply because you do not want to be alone. I personally believe it is better to be alone than to spend your time with someone who does not treat you well or pull his or her weight. Don't stay with a partner who makes you feel bad about yourself or does not contribute to the support of the relationship and family. *You need a partner who will be there for you whenever you need him.* You need someone you can count on during the down times as well as the good times of your relationship.

HOW DO YOU KNOW IF YOU HAVE THE WRONG PERSON?

Men and women both can be susceptible to falling for a smooth, sexy, charismatic player or the bad girl/bad boy type. But these types of people never make a good partner. You can never count on them when you really need them. He or she tends to require much more from you than he or she is ever prepared to give back. The keys to identifying this type of person are:

- Observe him over time and make sure you are not just evaluating what you see on the surface. He is always cute, often exciting, and charismatic, so you have to go beyond that layer. It is important to understand who he really is and how he will treat you over time.

- Look for inconsistencies in what she says versus what she does.

- Check out his friends thoroughly and see what type of personalities, character, and integrity they have. You can tell a lot about a person by observing and talking to the people with whom he surrounds himself.

- Is she reliable, or is she always making excuses and promising better days are coming? (You seldom,

if ever, will see any follow-through or better days
with her.)

- He will often bring you little gifts when he fails
to live up to your expectations. Don't fall for it. A
cute teddy bear will not make up for not being able
to pay the rent or car payment or providing for the
family.

- Is she financially responsible? Does she pay her
bills on time and manage to have some extra left for
discretionary spending and savings? Your partner's
shaky finances can severely impact your quality of
life, as well as your mental and physical health.

- Is he always checking out other options and spending a lot of unexplained time away from home or
speaking quietly on the phone?

- Is she actively contributing to the relationship, putting a smile on your face and giving you peace of
mind and making you feel loved? If not, move on.

- Is he always asking for things yet never seems
happy when he receives them—but then turns
around and asks you for something else? Do you
find that he never seems happy or contented, no
matter what you do for him? He constantly takes
or wants something from you, but never gives
back anything tangible. If so, this is a gold-digger. A lot of times, the gold-digger will tell you
what you want to hear about yourself because it
will trigger you to buy or give him something in
response and inspire you to keep him. You appear to be more of a provider and enabler than his
soul mate. Don't let his smile, charm, style, good
looks, or great sex fool you.

- Are you are constantly rowing, and she is constantly watching you row by yourself? This could be a potential gold-digger. It takes two people rowing together in unison to make a relationship work, survive, and thrive.

There are many great eligible single men and women available in the United States and around the world. *Take your time, and find the right one.* Do not panic, and do not settle for less than someone who will make and keep you happy. Remember, you are looking for a good man or a good woman who wants to work with you to build something special, magical, and worth having. He or she may be a professional/career-minded or a blue-collar worker. He or she may also be the stay-at-home partner or the spouse who supports the family and kids from home. What really matters is that you find the right person to complement and enhance your life. You deserve it! No one is perfect, but there are enough qualified singles who can make and keep you happy if you give him or her the chance.

Now, ladies, I always tell my daughters and my female clients, "The only cute and sexy man is one with a steady job with benefits (health care, life insurance, pension, retirement savings plan, paid vacation)." There are a few exceptions, but after traveling all over the world, I haven't met more than a few men who work well in reverse roles. These guys are the primary caregivers for their family; they transport their kids to various activities; they help with their homework; they cook and wash clothes. Their wives have extremely demanding jobs and travel extensively in and out of the country. These men provide the anchor to their hectic lives and demanding careers. Yes, there are men out there like these guys, but be cautious yet open-minded. And avoid the guys who want to stay home, but don't contribute to the needs and care of the family and you.

You now know all of the considerations you need to make to determine if this person really is the right one, but ...

WHEN SHOULD YOU GET MARRIED?

This is the million-dollar question. My research and experience have given me a unique insight into when people should get married. I believe you should marry when you have:

- Found the right person to complement, enhance, and complete your life.
- Experienced a bit of life on your own, like having your own place and being able to support yourself.
- Reached a point where you feel you are not missing out by getting married.
- Done all the things you wanted to do while you were single.
- Made your decision concerning having or not having a family and the number of children you both want and agree to.
- Decided your life will be better by living it together as husband and wife or life partners.
- Agreed to support each other's rights to your own beliefs, convictions, and philosophy

When you are both sure that you have met the listed criteria, the rest will take care of itself. If you have reached this stage in your relationship and the fires are still burning bright, relax—you are well on your way to creating a happy and successful life together.

SUMMARY

Let's review all the key recommendations we have discussed so far. They will work for you, if you follow them.

- It is important to find the right person who complements, enhances, and completes you and your life. Please do not settle for anything less.

- If you are not sure you have the right person or it does not feel quite right for you, do not be afraid to cast a wider net and date more people. It is an infinitely better option than committing to the wrong person.

- Be open to going through a number of dates before you find the right partner.

- Keep reviewing your compatibility partner profile and ensure you are looking for someone who really exists. Some of you are looking for people that God hasn't invented yet or even thought to do so.

- The greatest adventure of your life is waiting for you. Search hard for the right person. And do not forget: you may have to travel or even relocate to find that person. I did!

CHAPTER 10

The Importance of Communication

Most relationships fail due to poor communication and a lack of empathy. Why do I say this? If you do not communicate, you keep your partner unaware or guessing about what is wrong. How many times have you applied the silent treatment to your partner? Often, your partner is unaware of why you are not communicating. And because you are not clearing the air by communicating, your partner could also be misreading you and your intention.

Good communication helps you build and maintain a lasting relationship. Let me introduce you to my friend Linda. Her story will show you why clear communication is critical to the health of any relationship.

Linda's long-time boyfriend would come to her place every morning to have breakfast. Linda was so poor at the time that she lived in a rented room. Linda could not afford much for food and only had a small refrigerator, where she kept a carton of milk and some grapes.

Every morning her boyfriend would come and eat her cereal and milk and drink her coffee. This continued for months, and she felt he was taking advantage of her.

He had a great job, a hot new car, and a big apartment, but instead of bringing breakfast or coffee or anything at all, he would eat the little she had. One morning she'd had enough and broke up with him. She told him he knew how much she struggled. She didn't expect him to pay for anything, because she was an independent woman, but she couldn't stand his coming by every morning and eating the little bit she had. She told him that he was inconsiderate and selfish, and she'd had enough.

He left and immediately purchased groceries and doughnuts and came back to Linda's. Linda opened the door, took the groceries, said thank you, and then slammed the door. He stood outside her door and cried and wouldn't leave. Later that day, she checked, and he was still there. So she dressed up in a cute outfit, and did her hair and makeup as if she had somewhere to go—she didn't. She opened the door and said, "Oh, are you still here?"

He asked if they could take a walk and begged her to take him back. He did not understand what was going on until he realized he could lose her. After that, he started to share in the responsibilities of their relationship and really demonstrated how much he cared for and loved her. They eventually married. Now he owns his own medical practice where she works and runs his office. They do everything with and for each other.

Sometimes all it takes is for the other person to realize that he or she could lose you. In Linda's case, better communication could have prevented the blow-up argument and breakup. Her boyfriend thought she did not want any assistance from him because she always talked about how independent she was. She thought he should at least contribute to her grocery bill. Neither one understood the desires and intentions of the other.

THE IMPORTANCE OF COMMUNICATION

Do not wait until your frustration swells before you talk to your partner about something he or she is doing or not doing that annoys you. You will save both of you the aggravation of another argument; it can be avoided with better communication and setting clear expectations up front. Good communication starts with the commitment to each other to keep the lines of communication open and flowing—no matter what. This is especially true when you are annoyed or angry with your partner. Question each other when you sense something is not quite right between you. I recommend you be an active listener and also pay attention to the non-verbal communication from your partner. Determine if her words are matching her body language.

Remember, the eyes never lie! When your partner tells you not to worry about something and that everything is all right, is it really all right? Look into her eyes and see what they are communicating to you. The issue may seem unimportant to you, but it may be critically important to your partner. You are obligated to listen and try to understand the issue and to work collectively to resolve whatever it is to mutual satisfaction.

If you take the time to know what is important to each other, it becomes easier to address it. You should never let friends and family come between you two—be very clear with each other on this point. Some family members may be self-proclaimed authorities on relationships. You have to resist listening to their advice and learn to take care of your own business together—keep other people out of your relationship.

If you have an unhealthy relationship, you can expect that your family members will try to help you figure out what is best for you—and that is different from letting family come between you. I suggest that if you need out-side advice to help you through rough patches in your relationship or marriage, seek professional counselors or the advice of friends or family who have relationships you admire. They have the benefit of wisdom gained from experience.

I want to make one other important point here: *Learn to fight without hurting each other.* Do not use harsh or curse words at each other. And never let violence enter your relationship. It is a recipe for personal and relation-ship disaster. *If you are too angry to keep your cool, walk away and stay away until you can have a civil argument.* Some people say they like to get into a huge fight and then make up by having great, hot sex together. I believe if that is a regular occurrence, they may want to consider seeking professional counseling, as there could be deeper issues boiling under the surface.

Always tell each other how you feel about one anoth-er. *Your partner likes to be reassured that everything is good with the relationship and that you still love and care about him or her.* Don't miss the opportunity to reinforce this. If you have insecurities, deal with them, and do not give your partner a reason to feel insecure about you. For example, if you are self-conscious about weight gain, lose the weight. If you are upset that your partner continually looks at other people when he is with you, address the is-sue with him and let him know it bothers you. No matter what the issue is, deal with it up front. Do not let it linger and fester.

No man or woman likes to date or share a relation-ship with someone who lacks self-confidence. You have to be self-confident and be able to leverage all your abili-ties to achieve your goals. Your partner cannot build your confidence for you, but she can be supportive. She can help reassure you, but you have to take the initiative and fix the things that make you feel less confident. If you do not feel good about yourself, how can you possibly expect other people to feel good about you? Find a way to love yourself. Accentuate your positives and work on minimizing your negatives. Let me introduce my friend Pamela to show you the potential impact of not loving yourself.

Pamela is a sexy, funny, smart young lady. However, Pamela constantly complains about her body and features to her friends and partner. Pamela continually reminds them that she used to be really thin but never really liked her face. She thought she had gained too much weight and was no longer in proportion to her size. She also complained about the slight bump on her nose bone and her double chin. Pamela complained so much that she started to drive her friends and partner away. They couldn't stand her constant negativity about herself and found that her negative self-image actually made them feel anxious around her. Although Pamela was a very cute lady with a great heart, many of her friends stopped coming around, and she eventually lost her boyfriend.

You cannot possibly love someone else until you first love yourself. That doesn't mean you love everything about yourself, but it does mean you love what God has given you to work with. Have a plan of action for improving the overall you! No one can ask you for more than that. *Change what makes sense for you to change, and learn to accept and love the rest.*

If you keep your communication focused on talking about your dreams, your plans, your love, your family, and each other, you will continue to have a very healthy and rewarding relationship.

THE DOS AND DON'TS OF COMMUNICATION

A few basic rules apply when it comes to managing a relationship based on good communication and mutual respect. Do not let the day end or go to bed when you are mad at each other. This accomplishes nothing. It also causes you not to sleep very well, which can lead to another day where you might be more irritable and more prone to fight or be disagreeable. Take your time, collect your thoughts, and sit down together to resolve issues. You will be glad you did. Let me introduce my best friend Graham's story to demonstrate how serious this point is.

My best friend Graham had a fight with his mother over the way she treated his new wife. The argument got so bad that he and his mother ended up not speaking to each other. One night before bed, his wife, Sofia, expressed her thanks to him for sticking up for her with his mom. Even though Graham was somewhat upset with Sofia, he assured her that he supported her 100 percent. He also let her know what she could do to help improve her relationship with his mother. They were satisfied with each other and happy that they had agreed on a new plan of action for dealing better with his mother. They made love and went to sleep in each other's arms.

Around 2 a.m., Graham turned to Sofia, writhing in pain and unable to clearly express what was happening to him. Sofia rushed him to the hospital, where Graham died hours later from a massive stroke. Sofia was able to go on with her life because her last words with Graham had ended on a great note for their relationship and love.

Graham's mom, however, has lived over a decade now with the nightmare that her last words to her son were filled with anger and being unsupportive of his wife and their marriage.

The moral of Graham's story is: "You never know when something is going to happen." Never go to bed mad, and never let a day end with your being mad at someone you love. Communicate until you resolve the issues, and do not accept any other outcome.

You also have to know when to let something go. Pick your battles. I always advise my male clients that of all the potential fights they will have with their partner, they should pick just two fights per year to verbally fight with their partner. This is just to help them keep their self-respect and feel good about themselves. I also tell them that when it comes time to go to bed on those two nights, they will find out who really won those two fights as well. I've often heard my female friends say, "I'll show him who really won that fight when he wants to make love to me tonight. He will find my back turned and a total lack of interest."

One of the best strategies is to accept your faults and say you are sorry—genuinely sorry. It is okay to acknowledge your partner's point of view and listen to his or her concerns, even if you do not agree. Life is simply too short to argue all the time. Take it all in, breathe deeply, say you are sorry, and ask your partner if you both can move past this issue. It may take a follow-up with some flowers, a card, a nice lunch or dinner, or whatever you believe will put a smile back on his or her face. Remember, you love your partner, so it is all worth it.

Whoever is the one initiating the disagreement or verbal fight, once you agree to let it go or forgive her, please do not keep bringing it up—that does not accomplish anything. Consider following the "48-Hour Rule." After forty-eight hours, agree to not talk about the issue again, no matter what!

It is okay to argue. In fact, it is natural that you will disagree on some issues and get upset about some things. When you argue, however, please remember to respect each other. Avoid calling each other bad names or making potentially incendiary remarks to each other. The pain it can cause can linger long after the argument is over. You can argue without being verbally abusive, emotionally charged, out of control, or violent. It takes work on your communication skills and your ability to present your points in an effective manner. If you both go into an argument with the goals of doing your best to listen and accept individual responsibility, and you agree to do whatever makes sense to settle the argument, you will continue to build and enjoy a strong and lasting relationship. Remember, you want to keep your relationship full of love, mutual respect, and support—this is one of the major keys to building a lasting relationship.

And making up after an argument can be a whole lot of fun. After you reach agreement, turn your former anger into passion and show each other how much you still love each other. Put on Teddy Pendergrass's songs "Close the Door" and "Turn Off the Lights," or Michael Bublé's or Blake Shelton's song "Home"—and the rest will take care of itself. And if you really want to change the mood, put on your favorite Maxwell CD, and I assure you his melodic voice will transform you both to a better place.

The best overall solution to arguing is to avoid the argument in the first place by improving your communication skills with each other. It is certainly a better path than constantly arguing to resolve issues. Learn how to communicate as calmly and clearly as you can. You should have an expected preferred outcome and solution in mind before you begin your discussion. Then talk it out, work it out, and put it to bed forever.

THINGS DO NOT HAVE TO GO WRONG

Many people I talk to believe the natural or logical outcome for a relationship is for it to end in failure. They believe it is just a matter of time before it unravels. I believe relationship success is based on building a strong foundation and continually reinforcing it. Let me introduce a concept that I call "Ace the Relationship Test." People in relationships go through this process every day—knowingly or not. You may not realize you are being tested and graded, but you will certainly feel the results of your test when you look at your partner and wonder why you are getting a certain attitude from him or her.

Your partner tests and grades you every day, all day—even while you are sleeping. Your goal should be to ace the relationship test. He or she grades your poise and etiquette, your ability to dress to impress, your ability to impress him or her with the perfect date and your dating skills. Your partner is grading your ability to communicate, even through the difficult and stressful moments of your relationship. He or she is grading your sensual and lovemaking skills and your daily habits and their impact on your relationship. He or she is grading your ability and willingness to support your relationship and lifestyle, and your ability to help raise happy, well-adjusted children, if you have them. He or she is grading your ability to keep a job, as well as your ability to turn your job into a well-paying career.

Your grade on the relationship test may be reflected in a simple glance, smile, or comment. Sometimes it is communicated by a reassuring look and a sparkle in his or her eyes when you have really scored well. And sometimes, unfortunately, you flunk the test and receive negative feedback in the form of the silent treatment, curt comments, or a downright ugly accusation or argument.

This is simply life played out on the daily stage. The important thing to remember is that you must do your homework and prepare for your daily test so that you can ace the relationship test. The better your preparation, the better your understanding of the tests. The better your understanding of the tests, the better your execution on each test you receive. You both need to understand what you expect from each other and prepare yourselves to exceed each other's expectations.

Every day, your bosses, colleagues, and associates test your ability and skills to deliver whatever is expected from you at work. What you might not realize is that when you go home, your partner will test and grade your ability to deliver on whatever is expected from you at home and in your relationship. Don't be afraid to seek constructive criticism from your partner. Remember, he or she holds the answer key and decides what the criteria is for receiving an "A" or a failing grade.

So how do you ace the relationship test?

- Understand what is expected of you.
- Ask questions when you sense there is tension developing between you.

- Maintain your poise, and be patient.
- Do what you say you will do, and do it when you say you will do it.
- Anticipate your partner's needs and be there with a solution or workable approach.
- Help each other and work as partners.
- Continually show your partner through your actions why you were a great choice and why you are worthy of his or her love and attention.
- Let your partner know when you like the way he or she does something or when you don't like it when he or she does a particular thing.
- Don't yell at each other, or threaten, or harm each other.

There are many other things you can do to help ace the relationship test, but I believe if you concentrate on doing your absolute best, executing on the points I just mentioned, you will do well, and your relationship should flourish. Each partner should provide encouragement and positive reinforcement. When you have issues, work them out!

Relationships should have free-flowing communication and be mutually beneficial. The better you communicate, the stronger your relationship will become. The better you communicate with each other, the more your mutual satisfaction will increase.

TALK ABOUT THINGS THAT MATTER

You may be struggling with the concept of what constitutes good communication with your partner. I want to make a few suggestions to get the conversation flowing in the right direction. Consider reminiscing about the fun times you've had together, and talk about the things that make you both laugh and smile. This releases positive energy into your relationship. Talk about the things you have in common and work to build as much synergy as possible. Let your partner know how you feel about your commonalities. Do not be afraid to share and show your emotions. This especially applies to men.

There is so much you two can share. All it takes is a little creativity and the commitment to act. You could share books, music, recreation and fun activities, movies, art, magazines, hobbies, dreams, friends, family, and your idea of your future together. Sharing these types of things can give you endless hours of great conversation. I always believe you should talk about what you mean to each other and why you are so good for one another—this reinforces your relationship. Talk about what makes you happy and brings you joy and excitement. It can be something you have already shared or something you would like to do in the future. These are the types of things that help your relationship grow and make it last.

My wife and I love talking about our next date or vacation. We get so excited discussing when it will be, where will it take place, and how long will we stay. I am confident that if you talk to any woman about taking her on a date or a vacation, you will have her undivided attention. Women love to go on a date, even after they are committed to you in a long-term relationship or marriage.

If it is early in your relationship, you can talk about what type of relationship you both want. You can discuss whether you want to get married, live together, or just have a mutually exclusive relationship as boyfriend and girlfriend. Talk about where you will live or the perfect location to work toward for your home together. You might discuss if you will live together before marrying. And if you decide not to, discuss why you do not think living together is right for you. It is important to keep each other on the same page in your relationship.

Remember, if you decide to live together before getting married, set a definite date for the marriage before moving in together. Let me repeat myself one more time: *Men are less motivated to marry once they move in with their partner and receive all the benefits of living together.* Please take this one to heart.

Also take some time to talk about whether you want to live in a house, condominium, apartment, or townhouse. Investing in a home is probably the most expensive, long-term investment most couples will ever make. It warrants taking the time to decide what type of home is best for you two. You might want to sit down and watch HGTV's *House Hunters* or *Property Virgins* programs to give you some ideas. It's also an easy way for you two to gain insight into each other's taste and preferences.

I believe the most critical discussion a couple needs to have is the one surrounding children and building a family together. You should discuss and determine if you both want children. How many do you want, if any? When would be the best time to start having children? How will it impact your jobs and relationship? Now let me share how important this conversation is to your relationship as I introduce you to my friends Mary and James.

Mary and James met while in college. They had a whirlwind romance and relationship throughout their college years and decided to get married after receiving their first job assignments together. They were both staunch Catholics and believed very much in the church and its principles. After marriage, James brought up the topic of having children with Mary. Mary would talk in generalities about having children but never would commit to a time frame or to how many children they would have.

Mary is a beautiful, statuesque woman with the perfect figure, and she was very serious about maintaining her beautiful body. Additionally, Mary was extremely serious about her career and wanted to focus on locking down and advancing before she thought about having children. James, on the other hand, wanted a large family, perhaps up to six children. It never dawned on the two lovebirds that they should have discussed the topic of having children in significant detail before committing to marriage together.

In the end, James kept pushing Mary to put her career on hold and begin their family. Mary was not interested in putting her career on hold or sacrificing her beautiful body at this point in her life to have children. Also, she was on the fast track to promotion and working toward a stellar long-term career at the time.

Long story short: Mary and James eventually divorced and never had any children together. Their goals for having children and building a family together were incompatible. They could not reconcile their differences in this critical area, and it ultimately ended a storybook romance and marriage.

Make sure you have the critical discussions you need to have before you marry. Discuss the important points in sufficient detail so you both understand the other's expectations about children, building a family together, and the timeline for making it happen. It will save you a lot of heartbreak and future arguments.

My next topic has to do with religion—many people try to avoid this discussion with their partner. I do not recommend you spend a great deal of time talking about religion in the initial stages of your relationship, but if you are planning to commit to a long-term relationship and possibly marriage, you must have this discussion beforehand. Talk about how you feel about attending church services, and make sure you are in sync with one another. Will you expect each other to attend the same church? If you have different religious faiths, will you expect the other one to convert? How often do you want to attend church—weekly, monthly, several times a week? This is a very important topic to address before you get married or commit to a long-term relationship. Even people from the same religion like to worship in different ways sometimes. You want to be clear on each other's expectations and supportive of one another.

Now let me introduce you to my friends Ricardo and Claire and their love story. You will see how important religion can be in a relationship.

Even though they came from considerably different backgrounds, Ricardo swept Claire off her feet almost immediately after their first date. They fell in love and within weeks of meeting, they starting talking about getting married. All of their friends were in shock with the speed everything happened between them. Once their discussions began to center around getting married, they started talking about where they would get married.

Ricardo insisted that they marry in his hometown's Catholic church, and Claire thought that was okay. Ricardo then explained to Claire that she had to convert to Catholicism before they could get married and that she must also agree that they would raise their children in the Catholic faith.

> *Claire loved Ricardo more than life itself. She agreed to convert to the Catholic faith and then proceeded to go through and complete the entire process required for her conversion. Later that year, Ricardo and Claire were happily married. They now have several children, and they all attend Catholic services regularly as a family.*

Do you love your partner enough to make this type of commitment? Is she expecting you to make a similar commitment to be with her? These are the talks you must have before you commit to someone long term. How you plan to practice and worship your faith can have a huge impact on your relationship and marriage if you are not in sync with each other.

CHECK YOUR BAGGAGE

People often bring emotional baggage into a new relationship. This can weigh very heavily on your relationship, regardless of whether you're the one bringing the baggage or the one who has to deal with your partner's emotional scars. If you openly discuss the things that are weighing heavily on your hearts, you can work together to lessen the burden. This is what true partners do—they help each other heal and move ahead. *You must also realize when the issues are beyond your skills as a partner and then help your partner understand that professional help may be the best way to go.* This is a delicate topic but necessary sometimes in relationships. Be supportive.

TALK ABOUT SEX

Sex is important in a great relationship, but it also can contribute to the failure of a relationship. Let's talk about how you avoid some potential problem areas with your intimacy. You'll definitely want to discuss how you both feel about sex. I suggest you discuss topics like:

- Have you enjoyed intimate relations before?
- What do you like?
- What do you not like?
- What are your fantasies?
- How do you feel about incorporating toys into your sexual relationship?
- How do you feel about masturbation or self-loving?
- Do you enjoy adult magazines or movies? If so, what type?
- Are you confident and comfortable with your sexuality, or are you more reserved and need to take it slower?
- Where do you prefer to have sex?
- Do you prefer the light on or off?
- Do you prefer to have music playing while you are making love? If so, what type of music and which artists do you prefer?
- How do you feel about foreplay, both giving and receiving?
- What type of sex do you prefer (e.g., oral, intercourse)?
- Do you like role-playing and/or dressing in sexy, intimate clothes?
- Is there anything special or different that you like to engage in during sex?

I firmly believe if couples ask each other these basic questions and have honest, open discussions about their intimacy and sexual needs, desires, and expectations, they will have great, fulfilling sex lives. Making love to each other is one of the most natural and loving ways to express how much you love, care, and feel about each other. You want to take the time to get this one right.

To both men and women: You cannot expect your partner to be a mind reader or an expert on what pleases you. Please talk to him or her and help your partner bring you the most pleasure possible. That is what making love is all about. The more you clearly communicate what you need and what works best for you, the better your chance of having a great sexual experience with your partner. *If you are shy, communicate clearly using nonverbal signals that let your partner know that something he or she is doing is working or not working, or is preferred or not preferred.* Whichever way you decide to make your wishes known, communicate, communicate, and communicate! The rest will take care of itself.

POLITICS

Even though I recommend you stay away from discussions of politics, the discussions will inevitably come up. When this happens, respect each other's right to opinions and beliefs. Be sure you can accept your differences and support each other's beliefs, even if your partner does not share the same beliefs and political party affiliation as you. Don't let your politics adversely impact your love for each other and your family.

LIMIT DISCUSSIONS ABOUT WORK

Another hot-potato topic that arises in relationships is obsessively talking about work and the people you work with. When your partner asks you about your day, give only the highlights, not a three-hour discussion about your coworkers and your stupid boss. Obsessively talking about work can be overwhelming for your partner—and boring. Instead, talk about the things that really matter to your daily relationship and future dreams—these topics lead to much more pleasant discussions and tend to end on a happier note. There is no way to fix the problems you are encountering at work, unless you decide to make a change. When that time arrives, sit down with your partner. Tell him or her what you are going through, and ask him or her to help you come up with a plan of action to improve your situation at work or support you in finding a new job.

It's important not to treat your partner like a therapist by sharing all your daily drama. If you find that your daily pressures are too much for you, see an actual qualified therapist. It can work wonders for you and your relationship. Professional counseling is covered by most major medical insurance plans. You cannot get your relationship right until you first get yourself right.

SUMMARY

Remember that when you find yourselves struggling in your relationship, it often is due to poor or strained communication. Pull out this book and review this chapter again, and take my recommendations to heart. *My recommendations are based on working with and observing thousands of couples from around the world. I only recommend advice I have personally witnessed as working over and over again with successful couples that have loving, enviable relationships.*

- Do not let your relationship fail due to poor communication and a lack of empathy.
- See issues from both perspectives and then do the right thing.
- Be positive; people do not like to be around negative people.
- Do not leave matters unsettled or walk away mad; treat each day as if it's your last. Treat one another like you are a blessing to each other from God.
- When you have disagreements, sometimes you have to agree to disagree and let it go. After forty-eight hours, close the issue for good.
- Relationships do not have to go wrong; focus on "Acing the Relationship Test."
- Keep your communications focused on things that really matter to both of you.
- Set clear expectations for your relationship and make sure you are on the same page.
- Seek balance and harmony in your relationship; open and frequent communication is the key to success.

- Focus on creating a great sex life together, and talk openly about your needs and desires.
- Be willing to compromise.

CHAPTER 11

Expectations Are Changing

IT IS NOT OVER

When I talk to people around the world, I often hear comments like, "It's over for me. I am too old"; "I missed my window"; or "The right person isn't out there." I cannot believe how many people believe they have to marry or find a lifetime partner when they are young or they will be doomed to be alone forever. Well, let me tell you that is wrong. *It is never too late to find the right partner.* Just don't give up on yourself and your chances for finding happiness with someone who loves and cares deeply for you.

MARRYING YOUNG

Some people have an obsession about finding the perfect mate and getting married when they are very young. I believe the reason for the high divorce rate in America (roughly 50 percent of all marriages) is because many people marry before they are truly ready. When you are young and considering marriage, you are unaware of so many things that you should ask or consider with your young partner.

Often, you do not know yourself and what you want well enough to make a good decision. This can cause many problems when you are trying to decide on the right person with whom to spend the rest of your life. *It is very hard to choose someone to complement and please you when you do not know what really complements and pleases you.* You often hear young couples complain, after about six or seven years together, that they have grown apart. They haven't grown apart! What really happens is they mature and begin to understand who they really are, what they want, and what makes them happy. Then they wake up one day and discover their chosen partners aren't really the best complement to their lives, and their partners don't want the same things out of life as they do. The relationship often topples over after a few years of growing tension between the young couple. I want to introduce you to my friend Mark and his story about marrying young.

Mark first married at eighteen years old. He was sure he had the girl of his dreams. She was beautiful, sexy, and exciting. Once they were married Mark asked her what she wanted out of life. Shame on Mark; he should have asked this question well before he even thought of proposing. She told him she did not understand what he meant. Mark thought her response was a bit strange so he started prompting her thinking a bit. He said, "Would you like to get a job? Start to have kids? Go back to school? Develop some hobbies?" She wasn't interested in doing any of these things, she said. She just wanted to stay home, watch television, and hang out with her friends.

At the time Mark was the sole support of the family, with an annual salary of $5,200. This was in the 1970s, and even back then, $5,200 didn't go very far. They didn't have much money left once they paid the rent.

> *But Mark wanted the American dream of the large house in the country, several beautiful cars, three or four children, a successful and respectful career, money in the bank, and vacations in exotic places. He quickly found out his beautiful young wife did not share his dreams for their future. Mark was stunned!*
>
> *Their relationship began to unravel as they soon discovered that the only thing they really had in common was a great sex life. And Mark knew that great sex was not enough to sustain a marriage for the long term, no matter how good it is. They were divorced within twelve months.*

Mark learned a very expensive and heartbreaking lesson. You need to be sure you know who you are, what you really want, and what will make you happy before you start to look for a life partner or spouse. Also, make sure you know who your prospective partner really is and what he or she wants from the relationship. You need to understand what your partner wants to do with his or her life, and how compatible your partner is with you. Don't be afraid to get these answers before you commit. The problem when you marry very young is that neither of you may know the answers to these questions. You simply haven't experienced enough of life yet to figure it out.

The other issue you run into when you enter into an exclusive relationship or marry young is that you might not be at the point in your life where you can attract the right person. It takes a while to master poise and hone your etiquette skills, but these are things that can make you highly attractive to another person. Remember, he or she is also looking for someone to complement, enable, enhance, and complete his or her life. The more you have to offer, the better your chances are for attracting the right type of person. It is easy to attract a hanger-on type of person, but it is harder to attract someone who's upwardly mobile and going places with his life.

If you truly want to avoid a lifetime of misery and disappointments, stay away from the player, the hanger-on, and the couch potato type of people. They rarely deliver on their promises and rarely change their behavior.

Marrying young often means sacrificing the opportunity to pursue a professional career or completing your education. Unless you happen to be a trust-fund baby, most of us do not have the money to put ourselves through college or trade school. This means if we leave the nest early to marry young, there is a good chance we will have to take any job, just to make ends meet. Usually, one partner ends up putting the other one through school with the hopes that his or her turn will be next. This sometimes works out but not very often. This is certainly something to consider.

Sometimes couples grow apart due to the time spent away from each other as one tries so hard to complete his or her studies and degree. Also, it puts a strain on the other person because that person ends up carrying the lion's share of the work and tasks at home during this time, especially if there are young children at home. Additionally, the one going to school may be learning and experiencing more than the partner at home. This can sometimes feel like a gap is growing in the couple's relationship; the person at home does not have the same exposure and experiences as the partner. All of this, however, can be overcome with good communication, strong commitment to each other's education and success, and the willingness to sacrifice. Still, if at all possible, *it's wise to pursue your education and achieve your ability to take care of yourself* before *you get married.*

I believe people should marry after they can take care of themselves. Just in case things do not work out in the marriage as planned, neither will be stuck in a bad marriage just because he or she cannot afford to leave—that is a very bad position to be in and one that you certainly want to avoid with proper life planning and execution. As much as I hated going to school, the difference it made in my career, my finances, and my ability to care for my family was well worth the sacrifice.

If you commit yourself to another when you are too young, you deny yourself the experience of meeting a lot of interesting people and seeing what type of person makes you happy. Many people tend to marry what is readily available, instead of taking their time and exploring their options. Just think—I found my soul mate and the love of my life in Athens, Greece. I was born and raised in Washington DC. She was born in a small village outside of London, England. *You never know where the right person will be.* Do not be afraid to venture out. Travel and open up your possibilities. You may also want to consider studying a popular foreign language, like Spanish, French, German, or Japanese, and then visit those wonderful countries. You will discover a plethora of new possibilities that may pique your interest. You will not be able to make the right choice unless you have fully prepared yourself. Take your time—it's important to get it right.

BUT LIFE'S NOT FAIR

"Life's not fair! It's really hard to find the right person." I've heard this more times than I can count, and I always respond, "Anything truly worth having is worth waiting for and working hard to get it." The problem with Western society is some of its mores are out of touch with current reality. Western society supports men marrying women of all ages; there is very little stigma attached. No one raises an eyebrow when an older man is sporting a beautiful girl in her twenties on his arm. The world is a man's oyster in Western society. However, when a woman dates or marries a much younger man, she's called a cougar. Many people in Western society still have a problem with this, but not with the reverse, when a man marries a much younger woman. As society continues to evolve, men and women will be able to choose whomever they want to date or marry without any social stigma attached—providing their choice for a partner is within legal age limits.

EXPECTATIONS ARE CHANGING

Today, many men want a woman who has:

- Substance and is well rounded.
- Higher education, including college courses, college degrees, and professional certifications.
- Life experiences, including a job or career; travel; study abroad; and who understands something about the world.
- A career that enables her to support her lifestyle and can complement a relationship.

There still are the traditional-thinking men who want a woman to stay home and take care of them and their kids. They will always be there. But these men aren't necessarily the type of man that many of today's working and career women are looking for.

MUST ADJUST OUR THINKING

Today's women want more out of life than ever. They are evolving quickly and much faster than many of their male counterparts. They are stronger and waiting longer to get married or to establish lifetime partnerships. They are expecting more from relationships, from marriage, and just about all facets of their lives. They want to complete their education and establish viable, long-term careers and professional jobs. They want flexibility in their lives and do not expect to be forced into assuming traditional roles and expectations of the past. They want and demand help from their relationship partners, such as:

- Assisting with the household chores (both in and outside).
- Caring for and helping raise the children (including taking them to school, practice, and attending school events).
- Running errands (e.g., picking up dry cleaning, grocery shopping).
- More involvement with daily activities (e.g., cooking).

They usually make their own money and want to be treated as equals. Greater numbers of today's women are earning salaries and bonuses equal to men's salaries and even higher. They are achieving supervisor, manager, director, vice president, president, and CEO status at increasing rates. Many of today's women want a man who complements, enhances, enables, and helps complete them. They also want someone who shares their dreams, their hopes, and supports their beliefs, values, and career. They want someone who agrees on how they will accomplish their dreams and helps build a life together.

Even with the changes occurring around them, I believe many men are slower to evolve and may be holding on to a belief that may no longer be true in many cases. Today's woman is not the same woman of your mother or grandmother's generation. In many cases, she tends to be less traditional, more ambitious, more independent, and less dependent on men for her support. Often, she is higher educated, more career-oriented, worldlier, and less accepting of the status quo. In fact, she attends and graduates from colleges across the country at much greater rates than her male counterparts. This is especially true in the Black American and Latino/Hispanic cultures in America. Many women also have their own condos and homes, their own money and their own cars. Many have traveled extensively. Some even have housekeepers and nannies. Many are deciding to have children and seeking alternatives paths to have them.

Today's woman has more opportunities open to her than were available to women of previous generations. Many professional/career-minded women believe they can balance a demanding career, a loving husband, and co-raising their family.

I find that today's woman is used to being by herself but still prefers to have a complementary, loving, and supportive partner, providing he is the right partner. She is not looking to take care of a man who only can offer smooth conversation, a sexy smile, and a great body. She might date him, but she is not going to let him move in and marry her.

For men to maximize their chances of attracting and finding the right partner, they must adjust their thinking and expectations about women—especially today's women. Men need to accept that women are bringing more to the relationship than ever before. Men will have to step up and recognize what today's women are looking for in a man. This change in women's expectations creates a dilemma for both men and women.

For women: It means accepting the traditional role of women as homemakers, wives, and mothers; or it means going after a more complete dream of achieving your degree, having a career, becoming a professional, and being able to take care of and support yourself. If you choose the latter, it doesn't mean you have to dismiss the great things about the traditional roles of women. You can still live your dream as well as incorporate some of the traditional ideals of a woman's role as wife and mother. Your man's expectations just have to be modified a bit to bring him into the twenty-first century. Today's woman expects to have the type of life she envisions for herself, which opens up all sorts of possibilities for her.

Today's women expect men to take on a greater role in helping and sharing with parenting and assisting with the chores. Why? Because you have the same time and schedule conflicts as he does. Something, or someone, has to give to make it all work. *Many couples achieve that delicate balance between their careers, family, and home life, and make it work. It requires compromise and sacrifice—and taking turns.*

This delicate balance enables many couples and families to achieve a much higher standard of living. There are two incomes coming in instead of one. As men and women learn to accept the change in expectations and embrace the richness it will bring to their lives, our divorce rate and relationship failures will start to fall dramatically.

Now for men: This change in expectations means holding on to the ideals of your parents' and grandparents' generations and finding a more traditional woman who can complete you, raise your children, take care of your home, and support your career. And there are certainly women who want to be homemakers, wives, and stay-at-home mothers. They may be less focused on seeking greater education and careers in order to be there at home for their children and family. But their numbers are decreasing, as more and more women attend and graduate from college and trade schools across the country.

The alternative for men is to embrace the evolution that is happening and seek a life partner who not only can be a great wife and mother, but who also can have her own fulfilling job, career, and dreams for the future. If you believe that staying home all day, every day, raising kids is a picnic, just take off a week and stay at home by yourself with your kids. You will have a brand new appreciation for your wife.

Today's women are not standing still, and the best of the bunch are moving the fastest. Are you tired of chasing the girls sitting at the bar and in the smoky nightclubs? Let me assure you that the right woman for you is probably *not* in your local bar or nightclub. She is on the move every day, enjoying life, and doing fulfilling activities. If you want to find her you have to change your thinking and meet her as she searches her environment to find her life partner. Are you hanging out where the best women go to play and enjoy themselves? I'll bet you are not.

WHAT IS HAPPENING NOW?

Whether or not you currently accept the concept of changing of expectations, women will continue to evolve and increasingly pursue their education, careers, and dreams. A 2007 *Bride* magazine research study indicates that the average age of a woman marrying in the United States is twenty-seven years old. This is a major shift from seventy-five years ago, when many women were expected to marry in their teens. This also means there are a large number of great women out there to choose from who are stronger, more experienced, and more aware of what they want out of life and from their relationships.

Still, some women today will feel the pressure from society and family and decide to marry too early. Some of them will find successful marriages and the right partner. Some will end their marriage in divorce and will go on to seek more substance, more completeness, more confidence, and more happiness in their lives with future partners. Some will pursue their dreams of a more complete life and career—that includes marriage and family later in their lives.

I've noticed that women seem more open to selecting life partners and marriage partners from other cultures, ethnicities, nationalities, and religious backgrounds. This dynamic—or change in expectation—puts increasing pressure on men who seek the best partners from their own culture, ethnicity, and religious background. The more open women become to exploring all their available options, the more it will limit the availability of these women to more traditional men who want to marry someone from their own background.

Some men may evolve slower, but I believe they eventually will begin to explore all their different options. Some of them will continue to seek the woman who reminds them of their mother in every way—the traditional approach. Some of them will choose from the selection of more progressive women. Some will be more open to selecting partners from other cultures, ethnicities, nationalities, and religious backgrounds as well.

No matter what ultimately happens, men will find greater numbers of professional and career-minded women who will complement and complete them, as well as help them raise a family and manage their home. These women, however, will certainly demand a little assistance from their men with the kids, household chores, and family activities.

Women will find a greater number of men across many cultures, nationalities, and ethnicities who will be more open and appreciative of the progress they have made. Women will also find many more men who want the type of partnership today's women seek.

Let me introduce you to a couple of Neanderthals that I know.

> *Not long ago I spoke with a couple of guys who told me they couldn't be with a woman who made more money than they do. This was the most absurd comment I'd ever heard, and I explained to them that I have exquisite taste, so the more money my partner brings in, the more things we can acquire and enjoy together.*
>
> *These men are what I refer to as Neanderthals. Neither one of them made over $50,000 per year but wanted a life of luxury and fun. How much easier would it be to achieve their dream life if their partners also made $50,000 or more!*

Guys, please wake up! America's greatest prosperity and production came on the backs of women who left their homes and children to run the factories and jobs vacated by their men who were in the service during World War II.

For any couple to be successful, they have to function as a team. "TEAM" means by working **T**ogether, **E**veryone **A**chieves **M**ore!

WHAT DO WE NEED TO DO NOW?

We have to embrace that expectations are changing and see this as a winning change for our country, our people, our culture, and certainly for us.

For our ladies: Please give yourselves permission to seek happiness, completeness, marriage, family, and a career. You deserve it. Do not panic and marry too early. Do not settle for someone who is only "okay" because you think you can change him. *Remember: people do not change who they basically are.* It is more important to get yourself into a position where you can comfortably take care of yourself and do the type of things you like to do. Then you can be more selective, and you also will become much more attractive to the men who are right for you.

If you are over thirty and still single, please do not get down on yourself and think that your life is incomplete without a partner. Your best years and happiness are ahead of you. You never know when one of your family members, friends, or colleagues might introduce you to your true love and soul mate. Remember to cast a wider net, and don't be afraid to date a number of quality people before you choose to commit your life to one.

Everyone is irresistible to the right person! Consider changing your job or location if your dating scene is starting to get stale or unproductive. Explore all the options available to you. There's a huge world full of exciting, dynamic people.

When you really want something, you have to act on it. Let me introduce you to my friend Leona.

> *Leona has talked about moving from her large met-*
> *ropolitan city to Atlanta for forty years. She likes*
> *professional black men who are well educated, charm-*
> *ing, witty, and well traveled. But she kept meeting the*
> *wrong type of men in her metro area—married men*
> *and "players"—and believed there would be a greater*
> *selection of the type of man she wanted in Atlanta, a*
> *city known for having a very large black professional*
> *population.*
>
> *I hope she actually gets on a plane to Atlanta and*
> *increases her opportunity to find the right man.*
> *Sometimes all it takes is a change in location to effect*
> *a change in your attitude and to fill your heart with*
> *renewed hope!*

If you have lived and worked in the same place for years and haven't found the right person, do your homework, consider your options, and change your life with a new job or location—or both. Remember, you cannot keep doing the same things, in the same places, with the same people, and expect different results.

For the men: Please do not be afraid to embrace a more complete and complementary woman. If you are looking for a mother, with benefits, you might want to see a therapist to help you sort through this. Increasingly today's women are not looking for—nor do they appreciate—that kind of man. You should find someone who can help make the journey through life easier and exciting. She can help row the boat as opposed to watching you row the financial oars by yourself. I always found two oars in the water make the boat go much faster and steadier. It will relieve a great deal of the stress men have while trying to pull off their rendition of the American dream. They are burning out and suffering from nagging illnesses much earlier and in greater numbers than ever before. You need two people working as a team to secure and support a good life together.

You have to be ready for women who have greater expectations and higher aspirations but also want to help you reach your goals. You'll want to use and embrace every available asset you have—and a smart, educated woman with a good job can be a huge asset in your life. Learn to enjoy, respect, and love the modern woman. She is quite fascinating, stimulating, and inspirational. I found that if you deny women their dreams, you take away a part of their soul and lose part of their magic. A "little girl" exists inside of women. That little girl is the caretaker of her dreams, aspirations, and happiness. You have to recognize that this is a major part of who she is, and you must cater to her dreams or lose all that made her so special when you first met her.

With a strong, complementary partner, you can accomplish so much more with your lives. Just take notice of the men who have chosen this type of woman and ask them what they think about their lives. It is not always easy to make it work, but anything worth having is worth a little hard work to achieve it.

I want to introduce you to a couple who provide a wonderful model for love, marriage, relationships, and family. I believe they demonstrate daily how to balance competing and conflicting schedules and shared responsibilities; they make it work.

I never thought I would live to see the perfect married couple, but now I have. This couple embodies togetherness and a strong family. They had both achieved stellar educations and lucrative jobs. They purchased a beautiful home together. They are raising two beautiful, well-adjusted children together. They share in roles and responsibilities. He takes off from work to make time to attend and support their school and after-school activities. She also takes the time from her busy schedule to be there for him and their children. They still date each other. They still openly love each other. They talk about what is important in their lives and what they want to leave as their legacy to the world. They talk about volunteering for community services and helping those in need. They still hold hands and do the little things that excite each other after years of marriage. They are excellent models for how a man should treat and respect his woman and how a woman should treat and respect her man.

They have gone through financial role reversals and made it work. Once, she demanded the higher salary and brought in the lion's share of the family's income. Now, he has assumed the role of major breadwinner, while she spends more of her time with their children and helping American families cope through these challenging health and financial times. She also is a huge supporter of the American military's families and continually looks for ways to improve their lives.

They are the Obamas! President Barack Obama and First Lady Michelle Obama are perfect examples of changing expectations. They also are great role models on how to approach marriage, love, relationships, commitment, children, working together, and the sacrifice required for great careers and professions.

Regardless of your opinion of President Obama's political views and actions, he and his wife represent a great family model and a true example of a modern woman and a modern man who have learned how to appreciate what each brings to the relationship. They have used those skills to not only help themselves but also millions around the world. Study their relationship and family model. Watch how the president looks at his wife. When is the last time someone looked at you that way or you looked at someone this way? I believe we can all learn from the Obamas' loving relationship.

SUMMARY

Women and men are evolving as people and potential partners. This is a great sign for the future of happy marriages and relationships. Men and women also are bringing more to relationships to complement, facilitate, and complete each other than ever before. Many women and men are getting married later. Those who married younger and later divorced are now finding their way back into the dating and relationship cycle with more skills, dreams, and fresh expectations.

Women and men must realize that experienced, educated professionals and career people offer a great deal to each other. It is a lot easier to create a great life together when both people contribute to the financial success of the relationship and share the workload at home. It requires sacrifice and compromise.

Men must keep themselves in shape, attractive, young at heart, sexy, interesting, and desirable! Women must continue to keep themselves vibrant, young at heart, sexy, attractive, toned, interesting, and desirable. *Once you meet and engage in a serious relationship, you still owe each other your very best.*

I want to reinforce one more time that seeking a younger partner may not be the best approach. I ask that you open your aperture and let your lens introduce you to more great opportunities for finding true love, marriage, and creating a great life together. I also ask that you look for compatibility with your potential partner on as many levels as possible. It helps keep the relationship fresh, fun, and exciting for both partners. You don't want to turn around one day and ask yourself, "What have I missed by being married to him [or her]?" *It is okay to take your time to find someone and make the right choice—it is never too late!*

CHAPTER 12

Balancing Relationships with Professional/Career-Minded People

Many people I talk to tell me they would prefer to have a partnership or marriage with a professional or career person. It is one of the most sought-after relationships today. That is because most people dream of marrying the ideal person who can help them create the perfect life together. I caution that you should partner with and marry someone because you are deeply compatible, enjoy each other's company, and share common goals for your lives. And above all, you like each other.

I want to take the time to address the pros and cons of relationships with professional/career-minded people. You have to know what the expectations each of you has so that you can make it work.

THE EXECUTIVE/PROFESSIONAL RELATIONSHIP

Many executives and professionals believe having someone to share their life and help build their success is highly desirable. Therefore, the potential to match up with one of this group of prospects is quite possible whether you are a man or a woman. Where do you find them? How do you attract them? How do you make the relationship work to both of your advantage? It all seems quite easy when you think about the two parties involved.

However, experience has shown me that it is one of the hardest relationships to put together and keep together. There are so many pressures that these couples face that have nothing to do with money. Many Americans believe that money will solve their problems; I don't believe this. *Money and the things you have to do to obtain it may make you happy, but it might put you two at odds with one another.*

So what makes the executive/professional relationship different? Let's discuss what each person requires to make the relationship work.

THE IDEAL EXECUTIVE/PROFESSIONAL PARTNER

I have interviewed and worked with thousands of executives/professionals in my life, and I have compiled a list of traits that were common preferences for busy executives/professionals looking for a partner or marriage. Most of them want someone with the following traits and characteristics:

- Educated, well read, and good conversationalist
- Good listener and empathetic
- Coach, cheerleader, and able to constantly reinforce and build the partner's confidence
- Knows how to make things happen for the partner
- Well traveled or has a high desire to travel
- Likes to socialize and is comfortable in both formal and informal social settings; can work a room in a social setting

- Serves as the anchor of their home and private life
- Able to make a life on his or her own that will satisfy and comfort him or her while the executive/professional partner is away on business or spending long hours at work
- Fun, exciting, attractive, and appealing to others
- Understanding and somewhat selfless
- If children are desired, willing to spend a major portion of his or her time raising the children and supporting their activities

Additionally, their ideal partner should fit into and complement their professional world. He or she should be comfortable with making decisions and moving forward without a lot of input or feedback from the professional partner.

In some cases, their ideal partner has to be willing to accept that the relationship and children will compete for attention and time with their partner's career and professional obligations and goals. And in some instances, their ideal partner may need to be willing to sacrifice his or her own career goals, education, and aspirations in order to support his or her partner's success and career.

These preferences for an ideal partner may be indicative of the needs and desires of executives and professionals, but they may also be the preferences of anyone looking for a great life partner or spouse.

A TWO-EDGED SWORD

A desired relationship with a professional or executive could be a two-edged sword if you are not careful how you work out the roles and balance your time together and the expectations in your relationship.

On one hand, the executive asks his partner to be the perfect spouse, coach, cheerleader, facilitator, parent, and lover. On the other hand, that partner may have to spend many hours, days, weeks, and holidays alone due to the executive's career obligations and commitments.

Some partners of executives/professional career people complain of having all the money and free time to enjoy an exciting lifestyle, but their partner is not free to be there to share it. They are lonely and sometimes feel a lack of attention from their partners when they come home because their partners are often too tired or preoccupied with work. They complain of receiving limited help with raising their family.

They often feel like they have to do everything themselves. They feel like their partner's career is more important to him or her than the relationship and family. They do not understand why their partner can't disengage from work, the computer, the cell phone, and conference calls while he or she is at home. And they complain that vacations seem like an extension of their everyday, hectic life, rather than a relaxing, loving time together.

Some of you might be willing to make these sacrifices in return for the lifestyle, prestige, and security. But take your time and consider both the pros and cons.

WOMEN EXECUTIVES/PROFESSIONALS

My research and dealings with many professionals lead me to believe that men and women professionals often differ concerning the desired traits for their ideal partner. Even though they share many of the same preferences with men, women executives/professionals often are looking for some very specific traits in their partners.

In addition to the traits that most professional people desire in their partner, many women executives/professionals expect their ideal partner to be financially sound and earning money in the same range or above theirs—they do not want to take care of a man. Some of them want their ideal partners to be a professional or career person as well. They also want their ideal partner to have his own home, or be willing to move in with them, or help pay for a new home together. Almost always, they insist that their ideal partner share equally in the family obligations, such as household chores and raising children. And they definitely want someone who is understanding and supportive of their career and professional obligations.

Some of them, however, are looking for an ideal partner who can stay home and anchor their home and be the primary caregiver for their children. This is a growing trend not only in the United States but also in many other Western nations. Let me introduce you to my friends Kay and Brian's story.

My friend Kay met a great guy named Brian and quickly fell in love with him. He was studying to be an actor, and she was in law school. After graduating from college and enjoying a whirlwind romance, they married and began their life together. Brian started receiving acting parts in the local area and enjoyed practicing his craft and displaying his talent on stage.

Kay decided to enter the business world as a corporate lawyer. Not long after beginning work, Kay found there was tremendous potential for career growth and advancement in her company. She began working ten- and then twelve-hour days, sometimes including weekends. Her career started to take off, and soon she had her own team of lawyers to lead and manage.

Brian was still enjoying acting but Kay's career demands kept her away from home for long hours. She also had a hard time disengaging from work when she returned home because her job included international responsibilities. This required Kay to make and receive conference calls throughout the evening and sometimes well into the night. Still, Brian was extremely supportive and very proud of his professional wife.

Soon after they decided to start a family, their first son was born. Kay was thrilled with her new bundle of joy and loved spending time with him. However, the demands of her career and job kept calling her back to her professional role.

Brian increasingly dedicated more and more of his time to raising and attending to the daily needs of their new son. They balanced their life very well for a time, and then they had baby son number two. This put huge pressure on both of their careers, and they had to make a decision on what would be best for their family, finances, and each other.

Kay and Brian decided that Brian would stay home and raise the children primarily, and Kay would continue to pursue and grow her professional career as a corporate lawyer with an international team of lawyers. Brian used babysitters whenever he had the opportunity for a great acting part, but he settled into his role as the anchor of their home, children, and lives. They have been happily married for almost fifteen years now and have two well-behaved, well-adjusted, loving sons.

Professional couples are finding out what works best for them and their professional and personal goals and discovering ways to make it work. Brian and Kay are a textbook example of how two people can come together, support each other, and build a great, rewarding life together.

MALE EXECUTIVES/PROFESSIONALS

Many male professionals, however, have a very different view about the specific traits they prefer in their partner. They prefer their ideal partner to possess all the traits we discussed earlier in this chapter, but they also prefer different traits than some of the professional women are seeking. Let's explore the differences.

Some professional, career-minded men do not care if their ideal partner is a professional or career person. They are looking for someone who can be supportive of their careers and be willing to anchor their home and raise the children. Their ideal partner does not necessarily have to be college educated, but she should be well read, well spoken, and interesting. Many career-oriented/professional women tend to prefer college-educated and career-oriented partners.

Many professional men prefer a partner who is willing to travel, sometimes extensively, even if she hasn't traveled a great deal in the past. Some of them would like to have their partners accompany them on business trips but be able to entertain themselves until business is over for the day, when they can share time together.

Many professional men do not feel that their ideal partner has to necessarily be employed, providing she meets the other criteria. This may be particularly true of men who earn large sums of money and have extremely demanding businesses and private lives. They may be looking for someone who does not need to contribute financially to the family finances, but someone who can hold everything together in their demanding lives.

IT IS A DIFFERENT WORLD

As you can see, the desire, preferences, and expectations of professional women and men can be quite different—at times. It depends on the person and what he or she prefers in an ideal partner. The biggest challenge is how to make it work, long term.

Let me present three scenarios to show you what you have to do to make this type of relationship pairing work.

Scenario 1: Two Professionals

If you are a professional person looking to partner with or marry another professional/career-oriented person, then your key to success will be how well you two balance your competing careers and lives together. You will have to manage the potential professional competition that might occur between you. You will certainly have to compromise for mutual benefit and decide on what is most important. You will discover that finding enough time away from your busy professional obligations becomes paramount. This is essential to keep each other happy and content.

Once you figure out what is most important, you will have to determine how best to make it happen. You must work diligently on your private lives as well as your professional lives. It will be essential that you both share the responsibilities concerning your home, children, pets, family, and private lives. This is not easy to do, but it certainly can be done. When you love each other enough to make the sacrifices, you will ensure your relationship works and benefits you both.

Scenario 2: Professional with Stay-at-Home Partner

If you are a professional person seeking to marry or partner with someone who stays at home to manage your home, personal affairs, and children, life will still be complex. It will also require a lot of compromise and sacrifice. Most stay-at-home partners will not let you dump everything in their lap. You must be willing to share the responsibilities and provide outside help when needed. This may include nannies, housekeepers, lawn maintenance professionals, handymen, or pool service professionals. Your partner also needs and desires a life that is exciting and challenging. He or she is not looking for a life filled with scheduling and endless daily chores. Your stay-at-home partner might have chosen or agreed not to pursue a professional career, but he or she still wants a fun and rewarding life. You must be understanding and supportive of your partner's needs if you expect your needs to be met.

He or she might want to take a week off and just get away for some quiet time and relaxation alone or take a trip with a friend. You need to know whatever enhances his or her life and make it happen frequently. Communication is still the key to making your relationship work and managing the tension that sometimes creeps into it. I suggest you sit down and talk every day, even if only for a short time. It will allow both of you to unwind and hear what is happening in each other's lives. It also helps you to determine how you can best support each other if the stress is starting to creep in and nip at the harmony between you. You really have to stay attuned to make sure you are never taking each other for granted. If you just remember to treat each other as equal partners, the rest will take care of itself.

Scenario 3: Professional/Working Partner with Full or Part-Time Job

If you are a professional person seeking to partner with or marry someone who also works but not necessarily in a professional or career-oriented job, your challenges can also be special and require greater attention and understanding. The key to this type of relationship is to not forget that *your partner's job is as important to him or her as your career and profession are to you.* Many people's self-esteem, self-worth, and feelings of independence are tied to their jobs. You must respect this, even if his or her job does not seem as important as yours.

You cannot underestimate how much going to work every day can mean to someone. You cannot assume that because your partner's job does not pay as much as yours that it is not as important to him or her and the harmony in your relationship. It is definitely important to your partner; otherwise, he or she wouldn't be doing it. It is also important to your partner's boss and coworkers and friends at work. It represents part of their social network. People's social networks help bring them joy, and it fulfills a vital part of their life.

Having a job simply makes people feel good. It gives your partner something to look forward to and provides a way for him or her to contribute outside of the household. It brings your partner new experiences and things to talk about with you when he or she gets home. However, you will both have to compromise and arrive at decisions that are mutually beneficial. You will have to sacrifice some of the things in your work life in order to make both of your work lives work. But if you really care about your partner, your relationship, and happiness, you will not see it as a sacrifice but a natural part of being together as a couple and happy family.

You also cannot assume that because your partner does not have a career-type of job that he or she can easily take off from work. It's often harder to get time off from many non-career jobs than from some professional jobs. Every boss expects his or her employees to be at work, no matter what kind of job or career they have. Your partner's boss won't be any different in his or her expectations.

Of course, you will have to share in the home and family responsibilities since you both have jobs. You will have to work as partners to make your relationship work. You may even want to hire professionals to assist with childcare, pet watching, pool servicing, housekeeping, or lawn care. I believe this is extremely important if you want to optimize and maximize your time together for enjoyment. Nothing is worse on Monday morning than coming to work tired from a weekend of chores and overly demanding obligations. Get some help!

SUMMARY

Let's review some of the key points I would like you to take to heart as you seek the right one. Please remember:

- All that glitters is not gold. There is no short cut or guarantee.
- Just because something or someone appears attractive and attainable does not mean it comes without personal costs and sacrifices.
- Be supportive of each other's lives, careers, choices, and sacrifices; *no one's career is more important than another's*.
- Consider choosing a partner who complements and enhances your life, rather than competes with you and your career or job. When couples are both engaged in high-end careers or high-profile jobs within the same industry, it could put a lot of pressure on their relationship and sometimes lead to a very unhealthy relationship.
- Respect each other and be happy for one another's achievements and success.

This is the most important decision of your life! Take your time to get it right. Do not be afraid to seek professional matchmaking services that are reputable, hands-on, and discreet to assist you.

CHAPTER 13

Untangling the Mystery of Internet Dating

I believe Internet dating and matchmaking websites can be an excellent source for reaching more people who have similar interests, beliefs, goals, and aspirations as you do. Like any dating source, you have to do your homework and take your time to figure how best to work these sites to your advantage. My goal in this chapter is not to determine whether online dating and matchmaking sites are good or bad but to show you how to use them to maximize your opportunities for success. You can use these sites to find more potential compatible partners.

Why should you consider using Internet dating or matchmaking sites? The answer is very simple. The world of dating is changing at an extremely rapid pace. The traditional ways of finding suitable partners do not always work as well as they once did. For years, many people found their dates, partners, and relationships in school settings or in their work environments. These environments provide men and women access to a large number of potential partners. But if you have not found the right person at this point in your life, you may want to consider alternative ways of meeting new people.

First, realize that there still remain tens of millions of great men and women who have not found the right person. Fortunately, there are many avenues available that offer access to a large social network of potentially compatible people. The online (Internet-based) matchmaking sites are among the most popular.

I want to introduce you to my friends Michael and Joanna and their experience with Internet dating.

Michael and Joanna are your typical overachieving professionals. He was a busy professor working in a multinational corporation, and she was a medical professional. Both of them had achieved amazing success in their careers but longed to have someone to share their private lives and dreams. They had exhausted the traditional dating paths and became frustrated that they hadn't met their soul mate. Finally, they both turned to an Internet matchmaking site, and as luck would have it, the matchmaking site introduced the two of them. When they decided to meet, Michael took Joanna ballroom dancing. Michael was quite accomplished and actually was a ballroom dancing teacher. Joanna was impressed with Michael's ability to glide her across the floor and embrace her in ways that she had only imagined before. They continued to date after that first meeting. They have been happily married for over fifteen years and still enjoy doing the fun things that originally brought them together as a couple. Their tremendous love is evident to everyone that meets them.

Michael and Joanna probably would never have met without using the dating service. They lived in two different locations, worked in dissimilar jobs, and had no friends in common. But by mastering and trusting the dating site and their own instincts, they were able to put together one of the world's greatest love stories.

I am very impressed with the process matchmaking sites use to help people find compatible candidates. Some of the features they use can be better than what most people use during face-to-face introductions and dating. Internet matchmaking sites will force you to think about who you really are; they ask you to describe yourself in single words (shape: average; height: tall) and short phrases ("passionate about music"). They will also force you to think about what you like and do not like and to describe these things in single words and short phrases. Additionally, for you to use these sites successfully you will have to determine what likes and dislikes you prefer for your ideal partner, as well as posting your preferences into your ideal partner profile. This will improve the quality of your responses and potential connections.

Become comfortable with these types of profile activities in your everyday life, whether you are meeting people face-to-face or using an online dating service. You should always know what you are looking for and what you can offer to a potential relationship partner. Remember to exercise caution at the first meeting, and let a close friend or family member know who you are meeting and where. It is just a good safety practice.

THE SECRET SAUCE

The Internet dating and matchmaking companies all claim to have the "secret sauce" that will lead you to the perfect candidates. Some people have enjoyed success in using these sites. They learned how the Internet dating game worked and then mastered it to find the right person. But some people have had less success than they imagined with matchmaking services. There are various reasons why some are successful and some are not.

I believe the biggest problem with many but not all online dating sites is that they:

- Take away some of your most effective assets of attraction—your eyes, your voice, your smile, your body language. You have to learn to impress someone via e-mail and instant messaging as opposed to talking face-to-face.

- Cannot guarantee that the person you think you are communicating with is genuine; safety and identity fraud can become an issue.

- Do not provide safe, well-thought-out venues where you can meet potentially compatible candidates.

- Do not provide a personal touch, like one-on-one, face-to-face coaching to assist you in untangling the mystery of Internet dating and matchmaking.

- Do not always show you how to set up your profile to increase your chances for success. (Some do; some do not provide this service.)

- Do not filter out the serial daters, con men and women, and other undesirables so that you can gain access to the serious, compatible candidates.

- Do not tell you that you need to improve your dating skills as well as your communication skills to be more successful; and they do not assist you in doing so.

Let's face it: most of us never mastered the concept of the blind date. Now we are forced to use an electronic system we do not understand that requires us to apply new dating skills that many of us do not have.

Many of the dating and matchmaking sites are not intuitive and force you to use a trial-and-error approach to how to best utilize their features. If you do not have the time to do this, you might remain leery of whether this is a good way to meet the type of potential candidates you would like to meet. The other issue is the number of responses (e-mails, winks, instant messages) someone gets after posting a profile and picture on the site. Let me introduce you to my friend Dawn.

My friend Dawn is a beautiful woman in her late thirties. She is an extremely accomplished woman and a senior vice president in a global multinational corporation. Her friends often told her that she was married to her career and would never find a man. She did not have the time to look for or access to a good network of desirable candidates, so she decided to turn to the online dating and matchmaking sites to improve her chances.

After completing her profile and posting her picture, she received so many "hits" that she had to use a spreadsheet to keep track of all of them. After a very short time, frustration set in, and she tore up the spreadsheet. Some of you might say this would be a good problem to have, but nothing is more frustrating than taking the limited amount of time you have to sort through hundreds of well-meaning inquirers who simply do not meet your needs. It is hard to weed out any list for the candidates who lack chemistry with you. They may be compatible on paper, but they really do not have the chemistry you are searching for to make your relationship work.

Even though Dawn did not find the right person on the matchmaking sites, the experience of receiving so many hits let her know how desirable she really was as a woman and as a person. The experience helped her regain her confidence, and she began to approach life and potential relationships with a renewed sense that she could do it. She never went back to the matchmaking sites, but Dawn did find her soul mate and now has a handsome husband and beautiful son.

Some of you already have what it takes to be successful but are out of practice and need to boost your confidence. Dawn's experience allowed her to:

- Clarify exactly what she was looking for in a partner
- Improve her communication skills to the point that she could weed through potential candidates to determine if they had what she was looking for
- Grow her confidence. The experience showed Dawn that she was indeed attractive to a great number of eligible men. And that alone brought her swagger back.

I believe this can happen for anyone who still believes there is a right person out there.

I am a huge believer in creating personal and ideal partner profiles as part of your dating process. I highly recommend you do this whether you use online dating and matchmaking sites or not. This is the best way to get started toward choosing the most important person in your life.

If you choose to use Internet dating sites, it's important to know how the sites work and how to improve your chances for success. Some claim to have the largest success rate with bringing couples together in marriage, but they can't substantiate their claims. Others claim they have multiple, unique points of compatibility to help you select the best candidates, but they do not tell what the points of compatibility are or how they weigh each of them to ensure the best overall fit for each candidate. Let's see if we can untangle the mystery of Internet dating sites, beginning with the basics.

All of the sites ask you to fill out a profile about yourself and your preferences for an ideal partner. They ask you to upload your photos for potential candidates to view online. Some of them ask you to upload a personal video introducing yourself and quickly explain what you are looking for in a potential candidate. They provide you with all sorts of contact tools, including chat, private phone service, e-mail, and live video to assist in your communications with potential candidates. But none of them tell you how to put this new dating medium all together and make it work for you.

In the past, most people relied on face-to-face meetings, telephone conversations, and safe dating venues to get to know each other. Well, it is a little different with Internet dating and matchmaking. Your writing skills become your primary method of attraction and contact. These sites assume you are a great written communicator; we know this is not true for many people. So let's talk about the mechanics of how this all comes together.

WHAT IS ELECTRONIC MEDIA IN THE INTERNET DATING WORLD?

Most online Internet dating and matchmaking sites offer a number of tools to assist you. They include but are not limited to:

- **E-mail:** A simple way for you to send and receive electronic messages over the Internet. Most online dating/matchmaking sites provide you with access to their internal e-mail systems. These sites do not allow you to use your personal e-mail account and may block you from their site if you attempt to do so with one of their clients.

- **Electronic flirts:** Many dating sites feature the ability for you to send and receive electronic flirts to someone who interests you. The choice of flirts you can select and send are normally displayed on the dating website as a set of symbols. Eye winking, smiley faces, a pair of alluring lips, or a waving hand can represent symbols. You select the one that you believe will get you noticed and hope that he or she reciprocates or contacts you using one of the other available tools.

- **Instant messaging (IM):** Many people find this to be an effective way to get to know someone after making their initial online connection. IM allows you to talk to a potential candidate interactively over the Internet.

- **Video messaging:** Allows people to videotape a message introducing themselves and let's them describe who they are and what they are looking for in a potential candidate. This is normally prerecorded and then posted by the subscriber (you).

- **Web cams:** Applications like Skype allow people to visually see and talk to each other in real time. This is not normally part of the dating website but can be used by downloading the program from skype.com and using your web cam. The two people can be anywhere in the world as long as they have a web cam, the Skype application program, and a computer with an Internet connection and enough bandwidth to support the connection. Some sites have their own web cam enabler. Their online web cam facilitators allow their members to connect their personal computers and web cams via the matchmaking sites back-end program and bandwidth. This can be quite useful. But beware—some

UNTANGLING THE MYSTERY OF INTERNET DATING

people do not have good taste and may send you video content that you would prefer not to see.

- **Private phone system:** Some sites offer, *for an additional fee*, the ability to subscribe to and use an online private phone system to facilitate your communications with potential candidates. This is a good way to communicate with many candidates without compromising your personal cell or home phone numbers.

Internet dating tools also include old traditional media like cell phones, home phones, and pagers.

WHICH IS THE MOST EFFECTIVE COMMUNICATIONS TOOL?

The most effective communication tool for dating, particularly Internet dating, depends on many factors. You have to consider what type of equipment the interested people prefer to use, and what stage of the dating relationship they are in. Are you trying to establish the initial contact with someone online, or are you ready to get to know each other better? Some tools are more effective than others, depending on the stage of the dating process.

There are five basic stages to the online dating process, no matter which dating or matchmaking site you use.

- **Stage 1** – You are focused on attracting someone's attention and letting the person know you are interested in connecting. An electronic flirt may be effective, followed by an e-mail introducing yourself, with your best photo attached. Most people won't pay attention or respond to you without a photo. They will want to read your personal profile before deciding whether or not to respond, so be patient. Check your home page on the dating site to see "who's viewed you." That will let you know that they at least have enough interest in your initial contact to check out your personal profile and photo(s). Remember, the best candidates receive lots of electronic flirts and e-mails! You have to make sure you stand out from the crowd and inspire people to want to connect with you. One of my beautiful lady friends posted her photos on a dating site and instantly received hundreds of electronic flirts and e-mails from potential candidates. She had posted high-quality photos, and it paid off for her. It separated her from the masses and made her stand above the crowd. Posting quality, tasteful photos with your personal profile is the best way to attract someone.

- **Stage 2** – Once you receive acknowledgement from the person that he or she has received your electronic flirt, e-mail and photo, it is time to move to Stage 2. The person has indicated interest in communicating more with you, so you can now follow up with another e-mail. Be concise and genuine, watch your spelling and grammar, and please write to impress. Don't come across slick or too aggressive. Remember, you are trying to find out how many things you have in common and make your connection based on mutual interests and attraction. Keep your communications focused on these areas while showing the best of your personality.

- **Stage 3** – The lines of communication are now open. Your follow-up e-mail should be friendly. Talk about why you think you two would be a good fit. Discuss what you believe you have in common and let the person know you would like to get to know him or her better.

- **Stage 4** – If the person appears interested in what you have said so far and is open to communicating back and forth on e-mail, consider asking him or her to instant message with you. You two can have a more free-flowing style of conversation with instant messages and really start to learn more about one another.

- **Stage 5** – By now you should have figured out whether you like each other enough to actually want to talk on the phone. If you have reached this level of comfort, share your cell phone numbers, and perhaps meet for coffee, breakfast, or lunch at a *public place*. Meet the person there; do not give out your home or work address or phone numbers until you are absolutely sure the person is right for you and is safe. This can eliminate potential harassment if the date does not work out. Once you break the ice during your first date, you can then follow the normal dating and relationship guidelines detailed in the previous chapters.

Each one of the electronic tools can be effective in helping you achieve your goals in the dating process. The key is learning how to use them effectively. And that *takes practice*.

THE DOS AND DON'TS OF ELECTRONIC MEDIA

The best advice I can possibly give you is to take your time and plan your approach. You have to learn how to leverage electronic media smartly and to your advantage. Remember when you are using Internet-based dating and matchmaking sites, your competitive advantage becomes your ability to communicate in writing via e-mail and instant messaging. Posting high-quality photos also helps.

Think about how your selected media will be received by your intended recipients. Put yourself in their shoes and ask if you would be impressed if you received a similar message from someone wanting to meet you. You want to make your best impression with your first contact, just like you would in person. It is no different, except you are initiating your first contact without the benefit of your body language, look, style, and signature smile. This is why your photos are so important. Make sure your photos accentuate your look, style, and signature smile. This will help you make a great first impression.

Think about what type of electronic flirt would be the most effective at attracting the person's attention. You also should consider listing him or her on your "hot list"—almost all dating and matchmaking sites have a hot list function. This lets the person know you are impressed with him or her, because once you place the person on your hot list, he or she will be automatically notified that you have done so. Everyone is impressed when someone thinks he or she is "hot."

Please remember to be a gentlemen and a lady when you communicate with anyone over any media. We have already discussed how good manners and tasteful, well-thought-out comments can go a long way toward making a good impression. We also talked about how people like to communicate and meet with people who attract and impress them. I recommend you attach your most impressive photos to the e-mail messages you send to potential candidates. Do not ever, however, send explicit photos to anyone electronically. You never know where the photos might end up on the Internet. If your mother would object to the photo you are thinking about sending or using for your profile, it is probably not the right photo to use.

Your photo lets potential candidates see what you look like as they read your e-mails or study your personal profile. It can provide an edge for you against the other e-mails they receive (your competition). The combination of your e-mail and photo could be enough to get the person to notice you, gain a favorable impression, and actually respond. It is worth the effort.

Caution: Make sure your photos do not give away any personal information about where you live (e.g., house numbers or street signs) or what type of possessions you own (cars, jewelry). Check that the backgrounds of your photos don't reveal anything you wouldn't want the general public to know about you.

As mentioned, take your time to get to know someone using e-mails, instant messaging, phone calls, and web cams before you meet in person. Try to steer your discussions so the other person will open up about who he or she really is, what he likes to do, and what she does not like. You also want to discover some of his or her dreams, goals, and aspirations. This will allow you both to determine if you really like each other, enjoy talking together, and perhaps want to take the next step and actually meet in person. It is hard to tell if you have the right chemistry with someone without meeting and spending time in person.

Think of it like an electronic screening process that allows you and your interested party to vet each other. *It is not completely foolproof,* but it definitely improves your chances of success, while maintaining your safety. It also gives you time to check out what the person says about himself or herself and figure out if what the person has listed in his or her dating site profile is who the person really is. The actual person may be radically different from his or her listed profile and photos.

I want you to be careful—but not to the point that you build barriers between you and the potential love of your life. *Check out as many things as possible about the person before you decide to meet. This applies to both men and women.* Almost any point listed in his or her profile could be false. Many people tell me that in their experience, many of the candidates' photos are outdated and not representative of the person today. Candidates also love to falsify their age. My recent research of several dating sites revealed that many candidates falsified their ages up to ten years or more.

To counter this, I recommend you use Skype or one of the web cam/chat features available from online dating companies to video chat with a prospective candidate before you meet in person. This also gives you the opportunity to see candidates, as well as ask them to present their driver's license or passport to verify their identity and age.

Never send sexually suggestive comments to a person you are interested in. Keep in mind that many people may be turned off by this. It also sends a message that you are not taking the person seriously. If you are looking for a sex partner, go to a sex website, not a dating and matchmaking site. *The vast majority of people on dating and matchmaking sites are looking for someone they can take seriously and with whom they can have a potentially meaningful relationship.* These sites are wonderful for finding a larger pool of potentially compatible dating candidates than you have currently available.

In the early stages you are trying to build a foundation on which you two can build a great relationship. Once you get to know each other well and discover that you both like to play with sexually suggestive comments, please do it tastefully. And whatever you do, do not use your work computer for this kind of activity. Many companies monitor employees' e-mails that are transmitted on the company's network. Protect yourself from possible embarrassment and *keep your private life private!*

SUMMARY

- Internet matchmaking sites can be a valuable resource for finding great potential candidates.
- You are not alone! There are over 100 million single people in the United States.
- The key to mastering the Internet matchmaking sites is to understand how they work and then develop the skills you need to be successful with this resource.
- Your personal and ideal partner profile should be well thought out and brutally honest.
- Be careful, and confirm all the information potential candidates give you or list in their profiles. Some people lie, especially when it comes to relationship and marital status and age.
- Don't be afraid to ask for proper identification. This will help confirm age and identity.
- Verify the candidate's actual city or town and state. There are many scams on the Internet, particularly from overseas locations.

Most people list the actual activities and type of people they would enjoy meeting, but be sure to verify what they say against what they've written in their pro-files. Question any inconsistency.

For many people, Internet dating sites are a viable way to meet new people. Check with your friends for recommendations they may have for a particular site or company. Do your research first.

CHAPTER 14

The Seven Phases of Relationships

All relationships change over time. Some grow stronger and better; some lose their magic. It's important to understand how and why relationships change. This will help you ensure your relationship continues to grow stronger and retains its magic. I believe most relationships evolve through seven phases.

In this chapter, I'll answer these questions: What are the seven phases? Which phase are you in? How can you best maximize your success and minimize any chance for relationship failure?

The seven phases of relationships are the:

- Attraction phase
- Excitement phase
- Commitment phase
- Togetherness phase
- Waning phase
- Reborn phase
- Dissolution phase

I arrived at this concept based on my own experience as well as observation of hundreds of relationships. I also sought input from many of my friends and colleagues who have built, maintained, and managed lasting, romantic, loving relationships.

THE ATTRACTION PHASE

The attraction phase of a relationship is one of the most fun times of your life. During this phase you meet someone who piques your interest and it all starts. You think about how to break the ice to introduce yourself and really get to know that person. You might ask your friends, family, or acquaintances to introduce you or help you develop the initial relationship. You imagine what the person is like and if he or she would be a good date or potential partner.

Many things can trigger your initial attraction, but often it is:

- A physical trait
- His or her look
- His or her personality or charisma
- The sound of the person's voice
- The whiff of the person's cologne or perfume
- A simple glance from him or her
- The appeal of his or her outfit
- His or her smile
- His or her laugh
- His or her car
- His or her shoes
- His or her poise and etiquette
- His or her status or position (perceived power)
- Sex appeal

It doesn't matter what causes your attraction trigger to go off. The fact is you are intrigued, interested, and cannot wait to find out more about the person.

The attraction phase is where the chase begins. You start thinking about ways to spend quality time with him or her all the time. You constantly reflect on what you like about her. You try to understand the strong feelings and emotions you are feeling about him. You are constantly looking for ways to impress and motivate him or her to want to be with you. You look for any excuse to share time together.

The attraction phase is also when you might feel anxious and a bit tentative. You fear being rejected if you approach her or do not know what to do if she approaches you. You may start to doubt your ability to attract someone like this. Your confidence may be shaky. The attraction phase may remind you of when you were back in high school. You may act silly around the person, and your friends wonder why you are acting strangely.

I would like to share my story of how I met my wife, Pauline. It clearly demonstrates the attraction phase of a relationship.

Thirty-two years ago I was in the US Air Force, stationed outside Athens, Greece. Greece was a beautiful and fun place to live, especially for a twenty-one-year-old single man. But after the first year, I became homesick and thought I might go back home and explore the idea of marrying my old girlfriend and bringing her to Greece. I traveled back home but discovered she had moved on with her life, and we really were not a good fit. I got back on the plane and flew back to Greece, cutting my vacation short by two weeks.

Meanwhile, my roommate Patrick had met three beautiful young British girls at a local outdoor café. The girls were trying to find a good, affordable hotel. Patrick explained that Greece was a very popular tourist destination, and it was very hard to find a hotel during the summer season. He sent the young ladies to several hotels to check for vacancies but knew there probably wouldn't be any available.

The young ladies returned to the café very disappointed. Patrick suggested they stay at his home on the hill, not far from there, until his roommate (me) returned from vacation—he wasn't expecting me for two weeks. He only asked them to help keep the house in order in return for their accommodations. They thought it was a great deal and took a taxi home with Patrick. During the taxi ride, the ladies told Patrick that they were very nice girls and did not want any mischief from him or his friends. Patrick agreed, and the girls were relieved.

On the fifth day of their stay, after Patrick went off to work and left the girls to sunbathe and enjoy the area, I arrived home from my vacation in America—and discovered that I had lost my key. I rang the doorbell, hoping Patrick would be home, but when the door suddenly opened, a beautiful young lady stood in front of me. She told me her name was Anne and that Patrick had invited her and her friends to stay at the house. Then I noticed the two other young ladies running through the house in swimsuits. Anne said they were Cathy and Pauline.

I had never seen such beautiful women in my life. I got to know a little about them and discovered they were all single. Each of them had great poise and impeccable etiquette. I was immediately in the attraction phase. I loved their look, outfits, smile, eyes, and perfume. I just had to get to know them better.

Very quickly, I found myself staring at the stunningly beautiful Pauline. She had the most amazing curly blonde hair and green eyes I had ever seen. I began to notice that she smiled every time our eyes met. I found all sorts of reasons to spend time with Pauline. Whenever we all went out to party, I would stay close to her, focus all my attention on her, and do everything to try to impress her, even if it made me look silly. I did not care what my friends thought. I was smitten!

Have you found yourself smitten by someone and acting crazy, or found yourself chasing after the joy he or she brings you each time you're together? This is what life is all about. Everyone around you recognizes that you are attracted to him or her. This is one of the most fun experiences of our lives. But the next phase is even more fun.

THE EXCITEMENT PHASE

The excitement phase of a relationship is when you start to get butterflies in your stomach. You react with excitement every time you see him, talk to her, spend time together, and hear or think about him or her. Your friends wonder now what is wrong with you and why you are acting so strangely. They start to question why you are not hanging out with them like you used to. But you don't care. You are hopeful, excited, and filled with anticipation.

You find yourself spending every waking moment thinking about your new partner and developing your relationship. You simply cannot wait to see him and wonder what your next shared moment will be. You discover that you share and enjoy many common activities and beliefs. You feel like there is no one else in the world but the two of you. You are constantly holding hands, touching, kissing, nibbling, and creating magic moments together.

Everything seems magical. You are constantly surprising each other. You love focusing on doing the little things that mean so much to each other. You feel unbelievably happy, and it is very evident to everyone. Every time you meet, you discover another thing you like about each other. There is nothing you would not consider doing for each other. Life is simply amazing. You feel safe, comfortable, and at ease together. You just want to pinch yourself to prove you are not imagining it all. You discuss the possibility of your relationship becoming more serious. You are absolutely giddy.

THE COMMITMENT PHASE

The commitment phase is what many of us hope for and what some of us shy away from. This is the time when you both decide to formalize your relationship. You may decide to become boyfriend and girlfriend, or exclusive partners, or maybe even get married. You realize your partner makes you feel special, and you want her to be part of your daily life. You cannot imagine your life without him.

During this phase, you discover how many things you share in common. You spend the majority of your time together. You find yourselves spending time planning, sharing, growing closer, and just having fun together. Your lives have never been more exciting and promising than now.

You have general agreement on how you want to live your lives together. You have serious discussions about:

- Where you want to live
- Type of home you both want
- Division of responsibilities and chores
- Whether you both want children, when, and how many

You are excited about this phase of your relationship, but some of you will find yourselves worrying and feeling a bit of anxiety during the commitment phase. You may wonder if this is truly the right person. You may also wonder whether you should commit the rest of your life to this person. You find yourself wondering:

- What if it does not work?
- Will she break my heart or continue to be the loving and supportive person I now know?
- Will he be a great father? (Will she be a great mother?)
- Will she fit into my social circle? Will Mom and Dad actually accept him?

You also are very nervous and anxious about her possibly leaving you if you do not commit soon. There are so many things going through your mind that you may not be able to sleep well. This is quite normal and natural; this is the most important decision of your entire life so it is expected that your nerves and doubt will cause you to be on edge and unsure of this important decision.

It is also during the commitment phase that you find your friends and family offering advice about what you should do. If they like your partner, they remind you of all her great qualities and how great your life will be with her. If they do not like your partner, they will tell you everything negative they can think of to change your mind about making this commitment.

Find some alone time to steady your nerves, address your fears and doubts, and think through this important decision. It is okay to take a reasonable amount of time and compare your partner once again against your ideal partner compatibility profile. It is your insurance policy to help ensure you get this right. But at some point, your heart and instincts will tell you this is really the right person for you. Please remember there is no such thing as the perfect person, but there is a right person for you. Take the chance!

Will that really work? Yes! You will be able to gain your comfort level by remembering how he or she makes you feel and how much you enjoy your time together. If you find you cannot wait to be with him when you are apart, that is another indicator that this is the right person. If she makes you laugh out loud and smile to yourself every time you think of her and your life together, that is another good indicator that this is the right person. If you feel your life is finally coming together as you always imagined, that is a great indicator that this is the right one. But if these things are not true, please walk away, no matter how hard it may be.

So many couples get caught up in the moment and decide to move forward, even when it does not feel right inside. *Your instincts are one of your best filters for protecting you from making mistakes or putting yourself in danger.* Trust them. If the relationship does not feel right, do not move forward.

You have now completed all your evaluations, comparisons, and soul searching. You feel comfortable about moving forward to a more serious commitment. You start to get excited about asking or receiving a proposal to be exclusive, or move in together, or perhaps a marriage proposal. The day comes, and you commit to each other, and your life begins. You move in together. You celebrate a wonderful wedding and honeymoon. You are thrilled and feel like you are on top of the world. You pray every night that nothing changes and that it will only get better.

THE TOGETHERNESS PHASE

The togetherness phase begins when you two finally commit to an exclusive relationship. You are now back from your honeymoon, and it is time to put your lives together and function as one loving unit. You share everything during this phase of your relationship. You discuss your plans for building a future together. You begin to save for your plans for a new home, car, vacation, joint savings, children, daycare, and college funds. You put a timetable together for making these things happen.

During the togetherness phase, you are working extremely hard to keep each other excited and happy. *You still date each other and take vacations and **mini-breaks (extended weekends to fun places)** regularly together.* You continue to make each other your number one priority! Family and friends admire your undeniable happiness and your enviable relationship. You are so happy and never want it to end. Your childhood dreams of being wonderfully happy with your handsome prince or beautiful queen have come true, and you are living your dream.

Day by day, your plans begin to unfold. You start to acquire things on your wish list, and you are thrilled that you two made it happen. You are building a successful life and relationship together.

THE WANING PHASE

The waning phase is something that every relationship and couple will face at some point, but the time you spend in the waning phase can vary from couple to couple. This phase can be as short as a few weeks or months or as long as many years. *It is also quite avoidable*, if you stay on top of your relationship and keep each other as a main priority in your lives.

The waning phase is when you:

- No longer dedicate special time to be alone with each other.
- Stop expressing your love.
- Feel increasingly frustrated with your relationship.
- Start bickering over little things regularly.

Instead of focusing on each other, your children, friends, family, and work become the focus of your lives. *You stop dating each other* and doing the little things that once captured each other's attention, admiration, and love. Your sex life starts to become monotonous. During the waning phase you find yourselves looking around and noticing other people who attract your attention. Some of this is normal, but when you start to envision what a date, sex, or a relationship would be like with your attraction, you have crossed the line. Increasingly, you feel fed up, stuck, and more and more unhappy. You start asking yourself, "Is this it?" You talk about being bored all the time. You start to find fault and snipe at each other. Your communication is now filled with shouting matches, followed by the silent treatment. You know that your relationship is truly in trouble. Something must change. You may still love him or her, but you do not know if it is enough to hold your relationship together. In fact, you are not sure if you still want to be in this relationship. You start to think about your options.

THE REBORN PHASE

The reborn phase happens when you both come to your senses and realize how much you have invested in each other and in your relationship. You rediscover that you really *love and like* each other. You acknowledge that even though there are problems in your relationship, you still want to be together. You understand that your problems are solvable if you work together to address them and are willing to compromise. Now the work starts. First, you must realize that putting together and sustaining a loving, lasting relationship takes a tremendous amount of work, love, sacrifice, commitment, and compromise. It's hard, but worth it in most cases.

Once you come to terms with these realities, you start the rebirth process. You begin by opening the lines of communication and have honest and meaningful discussions about what is wrong with your relationship and the two of you. I also recommend you see a personal therapist to work out any of your personal issues and become the best possible you. Sometimes talking to a professional therapist and/or marriage counselor can help a great deal. You should slowly start to reintroduce the things that initially made your relationship work. You do things to reignite the crazy attraction you once felt for each other. You start doing fun and exciting activities together again and perhaps agree to begin a new hobby or activity together.

Let me introduce one of the hobbies my wife and I agreed to do together to give you an idea of how thinking out of the box can bring a whole new dimension to your relationship and activities.

> *I asked my wife the other day if she wanted to go to the shooting range with me and learn how to target shoot. She was absolutely thrilled by the idea. I know she secretly fancies herself as the next Caleigh Duquesne from CSI Miami. We have now decided to start taking shooting lessons together. I told her I was going to buy*

> *her a pearl-handled pistol, and you would have thought I was giving her a new diamond. She was so excited about the idea! This new hobby has given us something to enjoy together and expands our range of activities.*

Sometimes just doing something simple together can open up a whole new world of fun and excitement in your relationship. Start to think of the activities and dreams that used to get you both excited. Then begin to rededicate time for each other and the activities you want to do together. No matter how hard it is you must start blocking the increased demands by others for your time. I do not care if it is your kids, family members, friends, acquaintances, or job. You have to make each other a priority again and get back to the attraction, excitement, commitment, and togetherness phases of your relationship—and keep it there. If you can continue to cycle your relationship between these four phases, you will have a wonderful and lasting time together.

There are so many things that you two can do. Usually one partner pushes the other to try something new and the other resists. You have to be open to try new experiences if you want your relationship to stay fresh. Let me introduce a story about one of my friends. His story demonstrates how far some people are willing to go to reignite the fires in a relationship.

> *A friend's wife decided to take up skydiving. He's been reluctant to join her. I told him that he could either join her in her new pursuit for happiness or watch someone else join her and share in her happiness. I told him that he might even find a good compromise if he expressed his willingness to meet her in the middle.*

THE SEVEN PHASES OF RELATIONSHIPS

> *They might discover an alternative activity that they can enjoy together. When I spoke to her about how serious she was about learning to skydive, she said, "I'm so bored that I'll even jump out of a plane to wake up my husband and reignite our relationship and passion. But something has to change!"*

The moral of this story is that ladies are not waiting for men to change and stay in step with them. They are creating new lives for themselves and engaging in all sorts of activities and interests. As men, we must be willing to meet them halfway and be open to new things.

The next part is the true key to the rebirth of your relationship.

Once you start to date again, you find that you are getting back into each other. The looks and smiles you once admired have returned. You start to see each other differently and focus on the things you like about each other. You feel like you want to do the things to impress and put a smile on each other's faces once again. You begin the uncomfortable but much needed discussions about what is wrong with your sex life and reach agreement on trying new things. You are back in the exploration phase again of your sex life and look for new ways to excite, please, and bring pleasure to one another. You discuss introducing erotic toys, movies, books, role-playing, or sexy clothes into your sex life. Even though you are not quite sure of everything, you are committed to trying new things together.

You are excited about the potential of your renewed relationship. Your attitudes and positive energy begin to soar again. You start acting like two young kids in the park. You are not afraid to kiss and hold each other in public and among friends and family. All of them talk about what is happening between you. You discuss ways to prevent your relationship from getting into doubt again. You now have a new lease on your relationship and do not plan to ever lose it again. You are now reborn as a loving, dedicated, happy couple. Life is good—in fact, life is fantastic! Do not ever lose this feeling. It is what life is all about. Good luck!

THE DISSOLUTION PHASE

The dissolution phase occurs when you two cannot find enough reasons to rebirth and rebuild your relationship or marriage. You have simply allowed yourselves to grow too far apart. You stopped sharing activities and new experiences together. And you no longer feel the love and passion you once felt for each other. You simply feel like you must move on. You are no longer committed to making your relationship work and are actively looking for ways to end it and take your life in a new direction.

You may have hurt each other by introducing a third party into your relationship, and it has driven a wedge between you. You feel like you cannot get over the pain and hurt you have caused each other. You argue, fuss, and fight over the simplest things and do not feel compelled to work things out amicably. There are constant fights over just about everything, followed by the silent treatment and the slamming of doors and squealing tires off the driveway.

You may have betrayed each other's dreams and failed to step up to your promises. And now all you offer your partner are empty promises that fall on deaf ears. You have lost each other's trust and belief that you can share a good life together. Both of you are depressed and extremely unhappy.

You decide that enough is enough. You break up and move out of the same house. If married, you decide to file for divorce and begin the custody and child support battles, if you share children together. Your friends and family take sides, and things spiral downward and seem out of your control.

But why put yourselves through all of this hurt, pain, and negativity? Simply communicating together and making each other always feel special and a priority in your lives can avoid all of this. Sometimes relationships do not work, for whatever reasons. But before you give up on your relationship, give it one more try before walking away to be doubly sure you know that this is not the right person for you. And if that is your determination, then put together an exit strategy, line up your new living arrangements, secure your finances, get a good lawyer and accountant, and move on with your life. Life is too short not to be happy.

SUMMARY

- Relationships evolve, but that can be a good thing if you keep your love and relationship a priority.
- There are seven phases in relationships. You must understand what they are and what phase you are in at any given time.
- Avoid the pitfalls that cause relationships to fail.
- You want to keep cycling your relationship between the attraction, excitement, commitment, and togetherness phases.

- If things start to get off track, work to renew, re-build, and rebirth your commitment and relationship together.

- Don't walk away from your years of investment and hard work in building your relationship until you are absolutely sure that you two cannot and do not want to make it work.

- It is much easier to make your relationship work than to try to rebuild and recover from the pain and scars of a failed relationship. Look for signs of trouble and address them immediately, before they become uncontrollable.

- Remember, you were once crazy about each other. Make it last!

CHAPTER 15

Make It Last

I focused this book on how to attract attention, how to find the right person, how to determine if you have the right person, and how to make your relationship last. I hope you have benefited from my recommendations and suggestions. I want to use this final chapter to summarize what it takes to find the right one and make it last. It is something that you can make happen. It does not matter how beautiful or handsome you are. It does not matter how tall or short you are. It does not matter what your shape, figure, or physique is. It does not matter how old or young you are. But it does matter that you work on becoming the best you can be. This will open all the available options. You also must accept that there is nothing wrong with you and that there are many people in the world still actively looking for the right person. Your chances of finding the right person are great!

If you take nothing else away from this book, please remember that there is a right person for everyone—I really believe this. But more important, you have to believe there is a right person out there for you. You have to know what you are looking for, and you have to put some thought into it beforehand. You also have to do a reality check to make sure your requirements for your potential partner are realistic. After talking to many people from around the world, I truly believe if you put in the work to make yourself the best "you" possible, and your expectations for your partner are realistic, your chances for success are excellent. The more requirements ("must haves") you place on your potential partner, the harder it will be to attract and retain a partner. You have to bring as much to the dating and relationship game as you expect to receive.

But I do believe there are reasonable expectations that you should expect from a potential partner. There is nothing wrong with expecting your partner to contribute financially, emotionally, and physically to your relationship. There is nothing wrong with expecting your partner to help around the house with chores and help raise the kids and support their activities. There is nothing wrong with expecting your partner to keep well groomed and not neglect his or her physical appearance. There is nothing wrong with expecting your partner to have a job with benefits and to support your job and career. If one of you is lucky enough to stay home with the kids, or you do not need to bring in a second income, make sure you show your partner how grateful you are, each and every day. Understand that the one who goes out to a job is working for both of you. There is only one oar in the boat, financially, and it takes a little more effort and time to row the boat smoothly. Be understanding and supportive!

Make each other one of your main priorities in your lives and never stop that commitment. Continue to do the little things, and keep your lines of communication open. When you have disagreements, find amicable ways to discuss issues or walk away until you can. Never let your agreements spiral into violence or hateful words that cause you pain from which you might not recover. Remember you love each other, and you are expected to always respect each other, even when you are angry or have a disagreement.

Planning and attention to detail are the keys to pulling off a perfect date. Remember that when you first start dating, both of you will be nervous and want to make a good impression. Keep your conversation focused on each other and the things you have in common. You don't want to make each other work too hard to keep the conversation going. If you find that you really do not have any chemistry, then kindly thank your date and leave. If you are having fun and feel the chemistry flowing let your date know that you are having a good time and enjoy his or her company and conversation. Don't forget to compliment your date—and make it meaningful. Never stop dating—make it a priority in your lives. Don't be afraid to do something new and unexpected with your dating. Take the trip you always talked about. Get a chef to prepare a romantic dinner for two in your home. Share a picnic dinner in a beautiful park. Hire a limousine service and enjoy each other's company during the leisurely ride. Be creative.

Everyone should dress to impress. This does not mean you have to wear your Sunday church clothes, but it does mean you should dress appropriately for the occasion. Even a quick trip to the grocery store may render the opportunity to meet that special person—be prepared! Your poise and etiquette can give you a competitive advantage in the dating world. There are so many people who do not exercise good poise and etiquette that when a potential candidate sees that you do, he or she will be impressed and gain a favorable initial impression of you.

Please do not be afraid to commit to each other and give your relationship everything you have to make it work and last.

Women are demanding more from their partners but are offering more as well. Many of them want to have great jobs and careers along with having a family and children. An increasing number of women are making a higher income than their potential partners. This change necessitates that men be willing to take on a greater role with helping at home and with raising their children. It also requires both parties to be supportive to one another's career and goals. This will require sacrifice and a great deal of compromise to keep everything in balance and working well. It is possible. Men and women are doing it every day and making it work.

All that glitters is not gold. Some people believe if they date or marry a doctor, lawyer, professional athlete, or other high-end professional, their life will be great. This is not necessarily so. You have to date, develop a relationship, and marry someone for the right reasons. The person's job or career, in most cases, will not determine the success or happiness of your relationship. Some people believe having someone with lots of money or status is the key to their happiness. I have not seen this to be the case. The way someone treats you, manages the family finances, and takes care of his or her partner and responsibilities will have more to do with a relationship's success and happiness than having lots of money. I know infinitely more low-income people who are happy than rich people who are happy. There are so many more important things than money that are critical to the success of any relationship. Make sure your partner is bringing more than money to the relationship. If money is the base of your relationship, the future is not very bright, in my opinion. Find someone who has lots of things in common with you and makes you feel good just to be around him or her.

If you feel like you've exhausted all the traditional ways of finding someone special, consider Internet dating and matchmaking sites. They can be a huge source of potential new candidates. Remember the key to success with these resources is to post an honest personal profile and develop a well-thought-out ideal candidate profile (of what you're seeking). This will increase your chances for success. Post tasteful personal photos, showing you in formal and informal settings, will increase your chance of success. Please remember that people exaggerate in their profiles and may not tell the truth about their age or identity. This will require you to verify anything they have written in their personal profiles against what they tell you.

What does it take to make your relationship last? The same thing it takes to get your partner is the same thing it takes to keep him or her. Keep doing the things that excite each other, and keep your relationship fresh by introducing new fun things to do and enjoy. Keep your lines of communication open, honest, and frequent. Respect each other, and support each other's goals, aspirations, and careers. Help each other and share the responsibilities. And remember, all relationships evolve over time. Your key is to make sure you keep your relationship evolving between the attraction, excitement, commitment, and togetherness phases. If you find your relationship starting to wane, recommit to each other and start the reborn process. Your relationship and time investment is worth saving and fighting for. Above all, remember how much you like each other. Genuinely liking your partner and enjoying his or her company is often the strong base you need to rebuild your love (if needed) and make your relationship last.

I hope this book has challenged your thinking about men, women, and relationships. You now have all the tools necessary to become a great date as well as a great partner. You know how to execute a perfect date. And you know how to let your barriers down so that you become more approachable or feel confident enough to approach someone who catches your eye. You know how to communicate amicably. Above all, you know how to keep having fun together and make it last. The key from this point is to put it all to work in your life—and practice, practice, practice!

Your happiness is just around the corner. Good luck!

About the Author

After more than 20 years in the military and 16 in a corporate environment, Charles Johnson found another calling in life. In both the Air Force as well the many companies he founded or worked in, Charles managed and mentored diverse teams across Europe, Asia and North America. But he wasn't your typical corporate manager.

Charles always focused more on the whole person and how to help those who worked with and around him find balance and achieve both personal and professional success. He found that he was helping people not only get well-deserved promotions or the financial recognition for their work, but he also helped them identify and realize what makes them happy.

Helping others create a life and a lifestyle where their happiness is a priority and life balance is the primary goal became Charles' new life work. He became a certified life coach and author and founded AskDearlove Inc., a company dedicated to helping single people find and select the right life and marriage partners and make it last.

Surrounded by three sisters and eight female cousins, Charles had a significant female influence growing up. With the knowledge he gleaned from that experience, he spent the last 25 years coaching and mentoring hundreds of single professionals and up-and-coming, career-minded men and women -- including his own four daughters. He found himself providing guidance to help these otherwise successful individuals improve their personal confidence by updating their image, polishing their social skills and providing insight into the art of establishing and maintaining relationships.

Charles has connected and helped hundreds of couples find marriage or committed partners and coaches them on how to make relationships last. He has been married for more than 32 years and three of his four daughters are now married.

Charles has found happiness and balance in his own life as well, pursuing his passions as an avid traveler, photography enthusiast, art collector and a supporter of various charitable causes. He enjoys basketball, football and tennis. His greatest passion is writing about hope and how people can achieve their dreams and still have a balanced and complete life.